YOU CAN'T MANAGE ALONE

YOU CAN'T MANAGE ALONE

PRACTICAL PRAYERS FOR CONSCIENTIOUS MANAGERS

John S. Morgan and J. R. Philp

Illustrated by Lori Keene

Daybreak Books

Zondervan Publishing House
Grand Rapids, Michigan

Daybreak Books are published by Zondervan
Publishing House, 1415 Lake Drive, S.E.,
Grand Rapids, Michigan 49506.

You Can't Manage Alone
Copyright © 1985 by the Zondervan Corporation

Library of Congress Cataloging in Publication Data

Morgan, John Smith, 1921-
   You can't manage alone.

   "Daybreak Books."
   Includes index.
   1. Personnel management.   2. Employee motivation.
3. Inspiration.   I. Philp, J. R., 1944-   . II. Title.
HF5549.M635   1985   248.8'8   85-20226

ISBN 0-310-33602-3

All rights reserved. No part of this publication may be reproduced, stored in a retrieval system, or transmitted in any form or by any means without the prior permission of the publisher.

Unless otherwise indicated, Scripture quotations are from the HOLY BIBLE: NEW INTERNATIONAL VERSION (North American Edition). Copyright © 1973, 1978, 1984 by the International Bible Society. Used by permission of Zondervan Bible Publishers.

Edited by Julie Ackerman Link

Printed in the United States of America

85   86   87   88   89   90 / 10   9   8   7   6   5   4   3   2   1

CONTENTS

Illustrations	9
Introduction	11
Action	13
Administrative Assistant	15
Adversity	16
Advice	17
Ambition	18
Apathy	20
Appraisals	22
Assets	26
Attitude	28
Benefits	31
Bosses	32
Buck-Passing	33
Budgeting	34
Change	38
Commitment	41
Communication	43
Compensation	51
Complaints	53
Conflict of Interest	56
Conformity	60
Control	63
Creativity	64
Credibility	75
Deceit	81

Decision-Making	81
Delegation	89
Discipline	90
Doubts	99
Empathy	100
Fear	101
Feedback	105
Financial Analysis	111
Forgiveness	114
Goals / Objectives	115
Greed	122
Health Services	126
Hiring	127
Imagination	130
Inconsistency	133
Innovation	134
Insights	137
Interruptions	139
Job Descriptions	143
Job-Hunting	144
Labor Unions	147
Leadership	150
Loyalty	151
Managerial Style	152
Money	158
Motivation	161
Observation	163
Open-mindedness	167
Organizations	171
Paperwork	172
Patience	174
Perseverence	179
Planning	180

Potential Realization	182
Power	184
Praise	184
Privacy	187
Problem-Solving	188
Productivity	202
Profit	205
Purpose	207
Questions	208
Relaxation	210
Report Writing	211
Responsibility	213
Retirement	214
Risk	220
Security	224
Self-Appraisal	226
Self-Awareness	226
Self-Confidence	231
Self-Esteem	235
Span of Control	235
Success	237
Teaching	238
Teamwork	240
Time	243
Truth / Honesty	247
Wisdom	253
Workaholism	254
Worry	255
Index	258

ILLUSTRATIONS

Apathy	19
Decision-Making	86
Goals	120
Money	159
Problem-Solving	196
Relaxation	209
Retirement	218
Self-Appraisal	225
Self-Esteem	234
Time	242
Truth	246
Worry	256

INTRODUCTION

When you solve a difficult problem at work do you ever find yourself silently thanking God? Or when a problem remains unsolved in spite of your best efforts, do you enlist the Lord's help by praying, "Lord, if you help me out of this mess, I'll devote more energy and time to your work"? Or when you are under deadline pressure perhaps you pray, "God, if there were only one more hour in each day, maybe I wouldn't feel so rushed."

We have said these subliminal prayers on many occasions ourselves, and we suspect others have too. We pray because we believe it helps. With that conviction in mind, we wrote this book to give our prayers better focus and to make them more practical.

You can use this book in a number of ways:

1. Read it straight through.
2. Consult the Table of Contents. Every category has at least one prayer with commentary. Many have several.
3. Consult the index at the back if you don't find precisely what you need after checking the Table of Contents. For example, if you want a prayer that gives you spiritual reassurance, the index's notation on Reassurance will guide you to the Twenty-Third Psalm under the category *Fear*. Another example is vanity. The index reveals that a prayer about avoiding it falls in the *Self-Esteem* category. In addition, if you want to know what a mortal can do to supplement counsel from on high, consultants and others such as Peter Drucker, Eric Hoffer and Laurence Peter are listed in the index.

Try prayer even if you are unaccustomed to it. You might begin by asking for support in keeping these Ten Commandments for Managers:

Lord, help me . . .
1. Communicate both upward and downward with my people.
2. Manage my time more effectively.
3. Eliminate unnecessary tasks.
4. Delegate.
5. Manage by objectives.
6. Focus my relationships with employees on work, not personality.
7. Focus my own efforts on contributions I can make to work.
8. Coax the best performance possible out of my employees.
9. Fit jobs to people, not vice versa.
10. Concentrate on taking the right risks rather than on eliminating or minimizing them.

ACTION

Lord, see to it that I always do something because the only thing necessary for the triumph of evil is for good men to do nothing.

"The great end of life is not knowledge but action," said Thomas Henry Huxley a century ago.

Another Englishman, Samuel Johnson, said one hundred years earlier, "To do nothing is in every man's power."

The Bible has some sound advice on the subject as well.

> Go to the ant, you sluggard;
> consider its ways, and be wise!
> It has no commander,
> no overseer or ruler,
> yet it stores its provisions in summer
> and gathers its food at harvest.
>
> How long will you lie there, you sluggard?
> When will you get up from your sleep?
> A little sleep, a little slumber,
> a little folding of the hands to rest—
> and poverty will come on you like a bandit,
> and scarcity like an armed man.
> — Proverbs 6:6–11

Lord, don't let me just sit still; even if I'm on the right track, I'll get run over.

It came to pass that a man about to travel to a far country called his three top associates into his office. To one he gave responsibility for five projects, to another he gave two, and to another one—to each according to his ability. Straightway, the boss left on a business trip.

The associate who had been given five projects completed them so successfully that customers ordered five more. Likewise the one who had been given two completed them quickly and won two repeat orders.

But the associate who had been given one project did nothing. He sulked because the boss obviously favored his two colleagues over him. He reasoned that the other two, with more work than he, would not finish for a long time. So there was no rush.

Time passed so quickly and pleasantly for the third associate that the boss returned before he had done anything on the one project he had been assigned. The first two associates went into the boss's office to report first. He couldn't hear everything that was said, but he did catch the boss's booming cries of pleasure, twice saying, "Well done. You have performed so well with a few things that I will give you more."

Feeling desperate when his turn came, the third associate blurted, "Boss, I know you're a hard man. I feared I would make a mistake, so I held up on this project until your return. I need your advice."

The boss said, "My advice is to find a job elsewhere. This was a test, and you have failed. Ed will handle your assignment successfully in a few days. Around here, people who act get ahead. Those who don't act, even if they know how to, will get run over."

— Adapted from The Parable of the Talents,
Matthew 25:14–28

ADMINISTRATIVE ASSISTANT

> Lord, help me make my assistant a helper, not someone of secondary importance.

Some managers have had success with a "motivation through work itself" approach. This involves introducing new and more difficult tasks to a given job while allowing employees more freedom, decision-making power, authority, and responsibility. This approach also requires the reduction of supervisory checks and controls. The benefits are great: reduced turnover, greater employee satisfaction, better customer service, and more time to supervise.

When altering a job to give an assistant more satisfaction, ask the following questions:

- What do I do for this employee that he or she should do alone?

- What thinking can he or she do without my help?

- What goals should we set jointly?

- What advanced training should the employee have?

- What other job could he or she work toward? How can I help?

- Is there a way to combine this job with another that he or she would prefer?

- Is there anything the employee does that could be reassigned to a lower-rated job?

- Can anything that he or she does be automated?

Giving employees a wider variety of tasks with greater responsibility for their pace, quality, and work methods is an excellent way to combat disinterest, build more meaningful work, and enhance individual productivity.

> "Well done, good and faithful servant! You have been faithful with a few things; I will put you in charge of many things. Come and share your master's happiness!"
> — Matthew 25:21

ADVERSITY

Lord, when times are difficult, remind me that "prosperity conceals genius, but adversity reveals it."

Many have elaborated on the idea since the Roman poet Horace wrote these words. Here are some examples:

> Experience has taught me this, that we undo ourselves by impatience. Misfortunes have their life and their limits, their sickness and their health.
> — Michel de Montaigne, sixteenth century

> If you are too fortunate, you will not know yourself. If you are too unfortunate, nobody will know you.
> — Thomas Fuller, seventeenth century

> Adversity is the trial of principle. Without it a man hardly knows whether he is honest or not.
> — Henry Fielding, eighteenth century

> Let us be of good cheer, remembering that misfortunes hardest to bear are those which never come.
> — James Russell Lowell, nineteenth century

> To be willing to suffer in order to create is one thing; to realize that one's creation necessitates suffering, that suffering is one of the greatest of God's gifts, is almost to reach a mystical solution of the problem of evil.
> — J. W. N. Sullivan, twentieth century

> Though a righteous man falls seven times, he rises again, but the wicked are brought down by calamity.
> — Proverbs 24:16

ADVICE

Lord, let me take advice as readily as I give it.

When Aza Amaziah was twenty-five years old he started Software Track, Inc. to keep tabs on 27,000 computer software programs from 8,600 vendors.

At first he prospered mightily. *The Wall Street Journal* carried a story about his venture. *Business Week* interviewed him and carried his advice on how to start a new company: Begin with an idea that serves a business need; have enough capital; market aggressively.

Yet, Amaziah did not follow all his own advice. His rapid expansion brought over-growth problems—inadequate capital, overworked staff, and declining service quality that even aggresssive marketing could not offset. A key employee deserted him with two of his best accounts. He refused advice to cut back. He refused advice from the bank to bring in a partner who could provide capital and managerial experience. Instead, he found a stock underwriter who said he could raise capital for him through a stock offering. The stock issue failed. The bank called his loans.

When Amaziah was twenty-six years old he started all over. This time he did accept advice and took a partner who could provide capital and managerial experience in the ways of American business.

> Listen to advice and accept instruction, and in the end you will be wise.
> — Proverbs 19:20

AMBITION

Lord, save me from over-ambition.

In contemplating the implications of this prayer, consider what some famous, wise, or witty people have said about ambition:

> There is only one success—to be able to spend your life in your own way.
> — Christopher Morley

> Success is counted sweetest by those who ne'er succeed.
> — Emily Dickinson

> If one advances confidently in the direction of his dreams and endeavors to live the life which he has imagined, he will meet with a success unexpected in common hours.
> — Henry David Thoreau

> Success has made failures of many men.
> — Cindy Adams

> It takes twenty years to make an overnight success.
> — Eddie Cantor

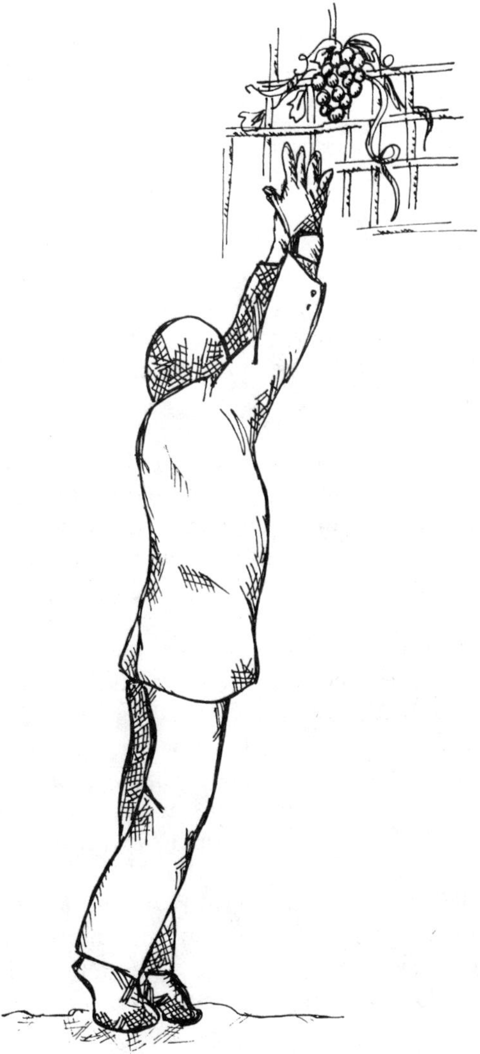

Six essential qualities are the key to success: Sincerity, personal integrity, humility, courtesy, wisdom, charity.
— Dr. William Menninger

Promotion should not be more important than accomplishment.
— Peter Drucker

Wealth is worthless in the day of wrath, but righteousness delivers from death.
— Proverbs 11:4

APATHY

Lord, please steer me away from sour-grapes attitudes.

Aesop's fable about the fox and the grapes has a contemporary counterpart in the workforce, and it is a major cause of apathy. In the fable, a famished fox could not reach ripe grapes hanging from a trellis. To hide his disappointment, he said, "The grapes are sour and not as ripe as I thought."

The contemporary version of this fable concerns Charley. He did not get the promotion (raise, assignment, or staff addition) that he tried for. Furthermore, he didn't get it when he tried again. The disappointments turned him into an apathetic time-server, saying to himself (and sometimes to his wife), "Why should I knock myself out? They don't appreciate all I do anyway."

Indeed, if Charley doesn't overcome his apathy he will prove himself right. It will become more and more difficult for his employer to appreciate him, and eventually he might even find himself without a job.

If you are Charley's manager, you can make special effort to accent the positive when dealing with him. Tell him what he does right; save up bits of good news for him; go out of your way to encourage him. If you must criticize him, do it in a friendly, not hostile, way. Tell him what he can do, not what he can't.

If you are Charley, here are some simple suggestions for avoiding apathy and overcoming a "sour grapes" attitude:

- Find a new job, either with your present employer or another one.

- Cultivate optimism. Emulate Thomas Edison, who said when the millions he had poured into an ore-milling process brought only financial ruin: "Well, it's all gone, but we had a good time spending it."

- Never let anyone realize the depths of your disappointment.

- Try again. Thomas Jefferson said, "I am a great believer in luck, and I find the harder I work the more I have of it." Maybe the third try will be the one that works.

If none of these cures your apathy, try the following remedies:

- For at least a week, keep a record of when you feel most energetic, when fatigue catches up with you, when you feel sharpest mentally, and the periods in the day when you are psychologically up or down.

- Avoid boredom because it relates closely to weariness. Temporarily set aside tasks that begin to bore you.

Or work on them only until you reach a convenient stopping point.

- Find good ways to rest. You don't have to be idle to relax. Turn to another task, change the pace, get up and walk to the water cooler.

- Avoid misusing your eyes. Your office or work place should have uniform illumination. Your eyes must adjust not only to your work but to nearby walls and windows. Monitor the intensity of your light. Several studies show that efficiency improves with greater light intensity—up to the glare point.

- Avoid clothing that is too tight or a chair, desk, or work bench at the wrong height. These may cause nagging aches and pains that distract you from working efficiently.

- Maintain your general level of health and have a regular medical checkup.

> The waywardness of the simple will kill them, and the complacency of fools will destroy them. — Proverbs 1:32

> One who is slack in his work is brother to one who destroys.
> — Proverbs 18:9

APPRAISALS

Lord, grant me the wisdom of Solomon and the patience of Job to appraise my employees.

Employees would be less apprehensive and more comfortable in their work if they knew how the boss felt about their individual performance. As a corollary, every manager has the responsiblity to know how each person is doing. Intuitively, every manager is, or should be, continually appraising.

Informal appraisal is valuable, provided it is done in a sound manner, without prejudice, and with complete objectivity. Set time aside regularly (once a week is not too often) to privately appraise all subordinates (only for your own edification at this time). This appraisal must be against agreed-upon goals, mutually arrived at with the subordinate. Then set aside a period (at least quarterly) to get together to counsel each employee about progress or lack of it. Keep this as informal as possible. Call it a progress report or anything but an appraisal session. Do it in a social context, such as lunch, and keep it short. If remedial action is necessary, agree upon what to do at these informal sessions.

A formal appraisal session (and call it that) should come at least once a year. The average employee wants it and expects it, like an annual formal party.

Lord, let me know how I'm doing by helping me create a mutually supportive atmosphere in which the employee feels free to tell me ways for me to be a better manager.

Lord, never let me mistake slogans for solutions.

Although a wealth of forms and formulas exists to help us appraise the performance of the people working for us, we should never succumb to a mechanistic approach to this task.

Instead we should use the "work-centered" approach,

which focuses on concrete and observable behavior, and the "person-centered" approach, which concerns personal characteristics of the individual under scrutiny.

> For in the same way you judge others, you will be judged, and with the measure you use, it will be measured to you.
> — Matthew 7:2

Lord, help me improve performance through control, measurement, and problem solving.

Evaluations must be planned and carried out in accordance with the following principles:

- They must be planned—what is to be evaluated, when, how, and by whom.

- They must be relevant in terms of purposes and objectives that relate to those of the organization.

- They must be objective, using measurable standards.

- They must be verifiable and reliable—confirmable by other evaluation techniques.

- They must be cooperative—among all involved.

- They must be continuous, although their form, focus, or emphasis may change.

- They must be specific.

- They must be quantitative, using numerical measures whenever possible.

- They must be feasible—administratively manageable and conducted without disrupting operations.

- They must be cost-effective—worth the expense incurred.

If I can remember these, I know I'll improve the performance of all who work for me.

Lord, let me promote employees on the basis of competence alone.

Much attention has been paid to the criteria and processes used in making promotions. Elaborate systems have been established to ensure that good decisions are made. We need to make sure that promotion policies and procedures in our own organizations are carefully written and available to all employees as a matter of policy.

Good performance evaluation is necessary for the success of an organization, as is an accurate prediction of an employee's performance in an unfamiliar job.

Performance appraisals touch on one of the most emotionally charged activities in business life—the assessment of a person's contribution and ability. The signals employees receive about this assessment strongly affect their self-esteem and subsequent performance. Therefore we must think through the human consequences of the procedures we set in motion. Good intentions don't suffice. Too often, in fact, we substitute good intentions for the hard work of analysis, with disastrous results.

1. Promotions should be based on an objective analysis of an individual's performance in the present position. Most promotional errors result from less-than-objective analysis.

2. Promotion should be based on the best possible prediction of an individual's performance in the new position. The best salesman does not necessarily make the best sales manager. Yet, we must base the prediction on something. One element is performance in past jobs. Another is an intimate knowledge of the candidate and the future environment in which he or she might be functioning. What present performance characteristics are relevant for the future? What personal characteristics are relevant for the future?

The most important and difficult challenge in choosing the best person to promote to a new job lies in identifying the most relevant performance and personal attributes that are needed in the new position.

And there's another important thing we can do—pray for guidance.

ASSETS

Lord, help me conserve my assets now, lest I lose them in the future.

The concept that a manager's most valuable assets are his employees has become such a cliche that the cynics have a field day with it. Cliche or not, however, it remains true. Ignore its verities at your peril.

The recession of 1981–83 lulled some managers into thinking their employees would stay with them until retirement. They learned the fallacy of such a belief as the recovery spurred job-hopping, causing a near epidemic beginning in 1984, especially among professionals with esoteric skills in high technologies.

Some turnover is inevitable, perhaps even desirable to keep new blood coming into the organization. Your job is not necessarily to reduce turnover, but to control it. Your challenge is to ensure that those you want to stay will stay. Your chances of keeping your best performers improve when you:

1. **Identify those you want to keep.** Distinguish those employees who are critical to your business success from those who are only marginal contributors. Such an evaluation is more often talked about than practiced.

2. **Identify what they value.** Pinpoint what is most important to your best people. Money is usually one such value, but often not the most important. Challenging assignments, recognition, and opportunities for advancement frequently outrank money as key values.

3. **Satisfy their needs.** Begin a deliberate program, in line with business objectives, to provide what important employees need and want.

4. **Get in touch early.** Open communication channels with top performers. Learn if they are getting what they value.

5. **Stay in touch.** Continue to monitor the values of your best people. Values often change, so be alert and adapt your policies to any changes you detect.

Above all, manage your top people as you would manage your best markets. Get to know them well, then stay in touch because they change.

An inheritance quickly gained at the beginning will not be blessed at the end. — Proverbs 20:21

ATTITUDE

Lord, help me out of this rut; it is nothing but a grave with the ends knocked out.

Marty, a maintenance man at a shoe manufacturing company, has been performing his job capably but routinely for nearly forty years. He seems to be above his job in education, temperament, and intelligence, but he never complains. He has become one of those nearly-anonymous employees that many organizations harbor. His employer doesn't know it, but maintenance man Marty sports a different personality off the job. He is actively involved in scouting, which takes up much of his spare time. Marty has become a district commissioner of the Boy Scouts of America, an unpaid position that puts an unceasing demand on his time and energy. He devotes an average of twenty-five hours a week to directing the work of twenty-two volunteer commissioners, planning and organizing Boy Scout activities at the local level, and working on regional and national Boy Scout affairs. Scouting claims most of his creative energies; his paid job requires only a small portion of the abilities he has to offer.

Jack, on the other hand, lives for his job, putting in so much time at it that his family scarcely knows him. Yet, he rises rapidly in his company and becomes chief executive officer when he is only fifty-four. He dies, however, at age fifty-five of a massive coronary.

Agnes, an executive secretary in a major midwestern bank, tells everyone—especially herself—that she welcomes retirement "to get out of my rut." Upon retirement, however, she finds herself bored and restless. She suspects that other retired bank employees are in the same predicament, so she organizes a retirement club, persuades the bank to finance a monthly newsletter which she volunteers to edit, and sponsors social activities that the bank also underwrites. She finds herself busier than ever, but happier than ever as well. Furthermore, the backaches that had plagued her for years miraculously disappear.

Marty, Jack, and Agnes all found themselves in ruts. Marty got out by supplementing his boring job with stimulating outside activities. Jack's rut eventually caved in on him, and he died. But Agnes, by melding her former work experiences into a new activity that became almost a second career, perhaps found the best solution.

Walter Pater, a nineteenth-century English critic, essayist, and novelist, wrote: "We need some imaginative stimulus, some not impossible ideal such as may shape vague hope, and transform it into effective desire to carry us year after year, without disgust, through the routine-work which is so large a part of life."

Lord, let my attitude surveys survey employee attitudes and not just make work for consultants and psychologists.

A financial institution had grown so quickly that company officials felt the need to take its personnel pulse. After checking the credentials of six consulting firms specializing in such surveys, they hired one. Although its $35,000 fee was the highest quoted, it offered to do the most thorough job.

And thorough it was. A team of three psychologists descended on the institution and interviewed about 100 employees over two months. Another two months passed while the consultants developed a battery of more than 150 questions for all 5,000 employees to answer on company time. (The original proposal stated that only a sampling of employees would need to be interviewed—not more than 400 in addition to the 100 that the psychologists had seen—"to set their parameters," as the experts phrased it.) The consulting firm also said it needed more money and time—an additional $25,000 and six months more because the initial interviews had unearthed serious attitudinal problems. The institution reluctantly compromised on $15,000 and three months more.

The final result: $50,000 in fees, more than 5,000 hours in employee time to answer the questionnaire, eight books of computer printouts cataloging the results by sex, race, creed, age, and other criteria. In addition, the company had to hire a new full-time employee to help analyze the results and implement personnel changes to meet some of the issues raised in the survey. The president estimated that the total cost of fees, employee manhours, and managerial attention to the procedure exceeded $150,000.

"And we learned nothing from the survey that we didn't already know or strongly suspect," he complained. "Furthermore, some of the solutions suggested by the consultants to remedy our personnel problems were not practical for our situation. For example, they said we should restructure our benefit program and offer more health insurance. That would have been fine for married employees with families, but forty percent of our workforce is single and under thirty-five. Instead, we went to a program we had been studying for nearly two years—flexible benefits, whereby employees can pick and choose from a 'cafeteria' of benefits to best meet individual needs."

Did the consultants do the financial institution any good at all? The president thought, then said, "They confirmed what we already knew or suspected. Maybe they caused us to take some actions we wouldn't have taken or wouldn't have taken as quickly as we did. But we could better have spent the $150,000 elsewhere."

> If you accept my words and store up my commands within you, turning your ear to wisdom and applying your heart to understanding. . . . Then you will understand what is right and just and fair. . . . — Proverbs 2:1–2, 9

BENEFITS

Lord, may our benefit plan satisfy our employees but not bankrupt our organization.

Major changes have occurred in benefit plans over the last several years. Significant changes are in store for the future. This prayer capsulizes the dilemma: How to balance employee needs against fiscal responsibility.

Consider the people problems. With a large population increase in the twenty-five to forty-four age group by 1990, there is likely to be more demand for programs covering medical reimbursement, time off, capital accumulation devices, and greater flexibility in the benefits.

These pressures plus inflation are bound to increase costs for employers. Inflation itself will lead to more demands for pension indexing as a protection.

To save costs, company contributions to benefit packages should be based on productivity. These may take the form of Scanlon-type programs (modified profit sharing where the payout depends on productivity gains) or awards of company stock.

Comprehensive medical plans are likely to become more common because they more effectively share the cost of medical expenses with the employee.

Specialized benefit coverage, such as dental and vision care, legal services, preretirement counseling, and preventative health programs, may decrease. More programs will require employee contributions.

To insure the future we must do a skillful and careful job of balancing.

> Use honest scales and honest weights. . . .
> — Leviticus 19:36

BOSSES

Lord, give me a boss who understands and supports what I'm doing.

> Some have bosses who must run their show.
> Some have bosses who don't care or know.
> God, give me a boss who understands
> I do my best with help, not commands.
> — John S. Morgan

BUCK-PASSING

Lord, help me graciously accept the fact that the buck stops with me on all problems I am responsible to solve.

Managers must establish and maintain the controls necessary to ensure the successful completion of tasks for which they are accountable.

Although they must often delegate to another employee the job of continuously monitoring progress, managers have the final responsibility. And the mere presence of controls does not ensure success, just as the presence of a fire extinguisher does not ensure the prevention of a fire.

However, managers should not shoulder responsibility for activities for which they are not accountable. There is rarely a problem where demarcations are clearcut. Troubles arise from ambiguous definitions and, much more commonly, from ambiguous responsibilities of employees who report to them.

A typical example of the latter is Mary, who complained to me that Ralph was goofing off.

"Sorry to hear that," I said. "I was unaware of it."

"That's because I've been covering for him, doing his work. Last night I had to stay an extra hour to catch up on the Smith job because he slacked off. It's the third time it's happened this month, and I'm tired of it."

"Let's go talk to him about it right now," I suggested.

She agreed, and we confronted Ralph. After his initial denials, bluster, and excuses, Ralph agreed to reform.

In this case the problem was solved rather easily, but

that's not always true. For instance, if Mary had been less specific about her charges (perhaps for fear of sounding like a tattle-tale) I would have investigated before taking action. If her charges held up after my investigation, I would have asked her to join me in the confrontation. If she had agreed, we would have proceeded as in the first instance.

If my investigation had not substantiated her complaints, I would have told her so, and asked her to report the next violation with chapter and verse.

If she had refused to join me in the confrontation even with specifics, I would have said, "Ralph will know you reported him because I'll have to tell him the source of my information. You might as well join me now as later." If she still refused, I would say, "If you change your mind, let me know, because he can claim that your charges are baseless if you refuse to face him. I can't go ahead without you because I can't rebut him if you aren't there."

By doing this, I am throwing the ball into her court. The complainer is responsible to back up the charges.

> He who rebukes a man will in the end gain more favor than he who has a flattering tongue. — Proverbs 28:23

BUDGETING

Lord, save me from budgets that do little but consume paper and waste time.

Budgets cannot take the place of good business judgment, but they are necessary. They represent commitments based on the most honest evaluation possible and formulated with the sincere intent to live up to them.

Sales budgets, the basis of annual profit planning, must be steadfastly realistic. Unsound reasoning or misinterpretation will cause loss and waste all down the line. Budgets should not be too tight, however; they must allow for change. Equally important are realistic and attainable objectives and justifiable standards. Because the annual profit plan represents "plans in action" and because the budgets represent the control of the operation, frequent readings must be made on them. Deviations from standards must be investigated, and corrective actions taken to adjust back to standard. Records must be kept, of course, to avoid similar deviations in future planning.

In most companies, each manager responsible for budget formulation is competing with every other manager for a limited amount of available resources (dollars, facilities, and man-hours). So work closely with your budget manager and justify your requirements so that your credibility holds up with your peers, your boss and, above all, with God.

Lord, keep me from trusting the fate of my business to the delusions of economists.

Most managers want to manage their own operations; they do not want to abdicate to some outsider. Unintended abdication can occur, however, if managers fail to budget properly.

Each year I remind myself of the following guidelines: 1) my annual planning for profits must be tailored for current conditions, not past circumstances; 2) it must be based on specific projections for my field of activity, not a broad guesstimate for the general economy; and 3) it must be based on the assumption that I am managing a new operation, not one I've been running for years.

Even in my organization where principles and practices of budgeting are understood, my wise budget manager approaches each new budgeting period as if the whole management team has to be re-educated in the intricacies of rational budgeting.

Although I detest the thought of putting the fate of my business in the hands of outsiders, I do not hesitate to place it in the hands of one who is not an outsider, as expressed in these lines from Psalm 16:2, 5–7:

> I said to the Lord, "You are my Lord;
> apart from you I have no good thing."
> Lord, you have assigned me my portion and my cup;
> you have made my lot secure.
> The boundary lines have fallen for me in pleasant places;
> surely I have a delightful inheritance.
> I will praise the Lord, who counsels me. . . .

Lord, save me from unreasonable budgets and budgeting unreasonably.

Budgeting is the part of the management function that relates to planning and control. Budgeting makes it easier to control short-range plans by involving all members of management, compelling them to set functional objectives and contribute to higher-level goals—profits, growth, and resources development. Budget discipline also makes it easier to measure performance because it compares goals versus performances on a periodic basis, using verifiable facts.

Budgeting brings additional benefits because it:

- Provides a basis for reassessing the validity of existing organizational relationships, goals, and product lines.

- Enhances cooperation, effectiveness, and synergism in preplanning.

- Orients management to a profit-and-result awareness in decision-making.

- Enhances awareness of detail and thoroughness in follow-up and heightens respect for records and their use in planning.

- Checks progress in achieving objectives; coordinates better teamwork of subordinates; identifies areas where savings can be realized or inefficiencies eliminated; facilitates the measurement of subordinates' performance; brings about a more realistic subordinate-supervisor ratio.

- Makes the most economical use of manpower.

- Defines organizational relationships and identifies relationships of authority and responsibility.

- Analyzes external influences in business, social, and political areas that affect the organization.

- Studies marketplace considerations that ordinarily affect only marketing-oriented managers.

> A prudent man gives thought to his steps.
> — Proverbs 14:15

CHANGE

Lord, make me willing to change even though it may cause controversy.

So much of life is changing, and changing so fast, that managers and professionals must learn to take change into account as a permanent factor in the workplace. Even more dramatic changes appear likely in the future. Those who deal with change most effectively, therefore, will fare the best in their careers.

Changes interact with other changes. A change that is primarily technological may force profound, but largely unforeseen, organizational shifts. Or a relatively minor change in the method of doing things—in selling, for example—may result in disturbing changes for people far removed from the selling profession. Be alert to the phenomenon of interacting changes, especially those involving technology, methods, organization, and people, the four most common types in the working world.

Technology. Many established companies have missed the boat with new technologies because they were unwilling to make changes or didn't see the need for it. For instance, at least two major firms knew about, but failed to pursue, xerography. Xerox Inc. saw the potential and created a corporation that now employs more than one hundred thousand people—technology interacting with people.

Methods. Changes in job design are common examples of shifts in methods that result in changes for people, too. The elder Henry Ford invented nothing, but his changes in assembly methods ushered in mass production.

Organizations. In managing change in an organization, the best strategy is to know how to spot the need for change, how to judge when it isn't necessary, and what you want the change to accomplish.

People. Probably the most complex of all changes are those that occur in people themselves. People generate changes in technology, methods, and organization, but "people change" is more complicated. It occurs on at least two levels—in social mores and in psychological mutations in individuals, due to age, changes in environment, or other factors.

Managing change effectively requires more than technique and strategy. It calls for a new kind of thinking about change. Change needs to be included as an element in planning, as a factor in all decision making, and as a pervading force in practically all other aspects of management. Think of change in terms of opportunity for self-motivation and progress, not in terms of displacement and disorder.

> Nothing endures but change.   — Heraclitus

Lord, help me understand that true progress preserves order amid change and preserves change amid order.

The great challenge to management today is to recognize and to respond effectively to the accelerating tempo of change that characterizes our society and economy.
— Orville E. Beal, president,
Prudential Insurance

The fundamental issue is to get managers to take time to step back once in a while and ask, "Do I really understand the change going on around me? Do I know how they're affecting my company? Where did this change come from?"
— Dr. Lewis Branscomb, director,
National Bureau of Standards

In business and industry, change is the price of health and vigor, and eventually even of survival.
— David H. Dawson, vice president, DuPont

The world is undergoing a transformation to which no change that has yet occurred can be compared either in scope or in rapidity. — Charles de Gaulle

These kids go to college and then to business school. By the time they go to work after all that schooling, they are twenty-five. In work experience they are the equivalent of the fifteen-year-old of a generation ago. But in theoretical knowledge they excel any one of their elders. So they go up fast—only to find themselves senior vice presidents at the age of twenty-nine but working for the same old bookkeeper I worked for years ago. . . .
— Peter Drucker, Claremont Graduate School

At the rate at which knowledge is growing by the time the child born today graduates from college, the amount of knowledge in the world will be four times as great. By the time the same child is fifty years old, it will be thirty-two times as great, and ninety-seven percent of everything known in the world will have been learned since the time he was born.
— Dr. Robert Hilliard,
Federal Communications Commission

Every new adjustment is a crisis in self-esteem.
— Eric Hoffer in *The Ordeal of Change*

What is new is not new because it has never been there before, but because it has changed in quality. One thing that is new is the prevalence of newness, the changing scale and scope of change itself, so that the world alters as we walk in it, so that the years of a man's life measure . . . a great upheaval.
— Dr. Robert Oppenheimer, director, Princeton's Institute for Advanced Study

Companies that take refuge behind the rock of security find that it soon becomes their tombstone.
— David Rockefeller, retired chairman, Chase Manhattan Bank

We are increasing the rate at which we must form and forget our images of reality . . . Change is the process by which the future invades our lives.
— Alvin Toffler in *Future Shock*

I think we are in constant danger—not from (change), but from losing our nerve.
— Dr. Robert A. Simon, Nobel Laureate, Carnegie-Mellon University

COMMITMENT

Lord, help me to gain greater commitment from people.

The dictionary defines commitment as a promise to engage oneself. Commitment to objectives is one of the strongest ways to achieve goals. While some authority is always necessary, authority rarely brings full commitment. What does? Let's look at some factors that could stimulate commitment, as first advanced by Abraham Maslow:

1. Man is a wanting creature. His needs and wants are never satisfied. If they are satisfied at one level—for example, hunger—new needs will take their place. Furthermore, satisfied needs do not motivate, but unsatisfied needs do.

2. When the physiological needs are satisfied—food, shelter, etc.—the next level of needs takes over. These are safety needs—the desire for fairness, freedom from tyranny and favoritism, assurance of fair administration.

3. Next are social needs—friendship, love, acceptance.

4. The fourth tier involves egoistic needs—self-esteem, good status, and wide recognition.

5. The highest level involves spiritual and other kinds of self-fulfillment.

Employers do well in satisfying the needs on levels 1 and 2, but progressively poorer from then on until the fifth level, which is rarely satisfied. On the third level, managers sometimes deliberately thwart needs for friendship. Some argue that friendship leads to cliques and divisive groups. But lack of friendship leads to antagonism, which scarcely encourages the full commitment of people.

Managers resist dealing with the fourth level, too. "Egoistic" bears an unfavorable connotation. We don't mean, however, that you should pander to conceit among employees. We mean that you should recognize your employees' needs for self-esteem and recognition. If you can give it to them honestly and legitimately, why not?

Managers face their greatest challenge in encouraging the self-fulfillment of their people. This is a private, individual matter. Of necessity, the manager's role must be limited to providing the proper conditions for self-fulfillment—an atmosphere wherein your people know they can advance on merit, know they have the freedom to err, know that better jobs await them if they do well on their present one, and know they are encouraged to bring all their spiritual resources to bear on their work.

With these factors in mind, you can build the proper climate to give orders and do the other things a manager must accomplish.

The most effective management style is that of those who appear not to manage at all. These managers so strongly motivate people, so skillfully build the climate, and so subtly phrase their requests that employees willingly carry them out almost as if they thought of them first. Indeed, the fully committed employee does often give self-orders.

COMMUNICATION

Lord, teach me to listen . . .

Supervisors spend an average of eighty percent of their time communicating. By far the greatest proportion of that percentage—nearly half of it—is spent listening. Of all the sources of information available to managers to help them evaluate personalities and potential of people in their departments, listening to individual employees is the most important.

Despite its importance, however, listening is neglected. University of Minnesota studies suggest that listening presents many problems. Most people remember only half of what they heard a day or so ago. Within a couple of months, they remember less than twenty-five percent.

Many factors contribute to listening difficulties, but these stand out:

1. **Inadequate background information.** The speaker overestimates our level of knowledge, and we hate to admit we don't understand.

2. **Selective inattention.** We hear what we want to hear.

3. **Selective memory.** We remember what we want to remember.

4. **Selective expectation.** We hear what we expect to hear. Sometimes, because of what we anticipate hearing, our minds record exactly the opposite of what is really said.

5. **Fear of influence.** We dislike having our biases, prejudices, and cherished beliefs upset.

6. **Bias against the speaker.** If we don't like who is saying it, it is doubly hard to hear what is said.

7. **Boredom.** "What were those previous six points the speaker mentioned?"

8. **Unilateral listening.** We absorb only one aspect of the speaker's message—the literal words, the connotation, the facial expression, or the tone of voice. To get the complete message, all four must be merged into a single impression.

What can we do to become better listeners? Fortunately, better listening can be developed—with an improved environment for listening, with proper emotional attitudes, and with sharpened techniques for listening.

The physical environment is to listening what the theater is to a play. No matter how intrinsically excellent the drama, it won't come across to the audience if the acoustics are bad, the props distracting, and the seats uncomfortable. Nor would a play be well received if presented at some outlandish hour.

Good listening also requires freedom from interruption, particularly from the telephone. If you don't have a secretary who can take your calls, get a device available in telephone stores so you can turn your receiver off. If the message is important, the caller will try again. If the person to whom you are trying to listen is on the phone and sounds long-winded, suggest a face-to-face session. Face-to-face communication is by far the most effective. In listening, seeing is almost as important as hearing.

An improved emotional attitude toward listening will help overcome seven of the eight barriers to listening—all but inadequate background information. If bored, conceal it. If you lack empathy, try to project yourself into that person's mind. What is the person really trying to tell you? What are the hidden agendas? A good broadening exercise is to take notes as the person talks, especially if experience has shown you that he or she can command only your narrowest attention.

The best technique to improve listening is to summon all your sincerity to the task. Act enthusiastic and, odds are, you will be. Besides sincerity, you can improve your listening technique by doing homework to overcome the first barrier to good listening, inadequate background information.

If the person wants to discuss a personal problem, take care. It's unwise—and usually unnecessary—to give personal advice. Most people with personal problems don't want advice; they want a sounding board, because talking helps them think through their problem.

In normal listening situations, ask questions when you don't understand. The speaker will be flattered, not offended. If you have been woolgathering and have hopelessly lost the thread of the conversation, ask the speaker to go back and pick it up for you. Note-taking will help you avoid this problem. Be alert when you listen. Don't slouch if you stand or slump if you sit. Never flatly contradict the speaker.

> The purposes of a man's heart are deep waters, but a man of understanding draws them out. — Proverbs 20:5

And teach me not to talk too much.

There is still another way to improve my listening habits, but how do I stop talking so much myself?

I know I must gauge my own verbosity, so I ask myself:

1. Do I explain my position in excessive detail?
2. Do I plan answers while another is talking?
3. Do I grow impatient while others are talking?
4. Do I often miss the other's point?
5. Do I almost always get answers I want and expect?
6. Do I often misunderstand certain situations?

7. Do I find gaps in my fund of work-related information?

If the answer is yes to just one of those questions, I'm talking a great deal, but not enough to seriously impair good listening. If the answer is yes to two, I must begin to watch myself. If the answer is yes to three or more, I need help.

Listening is like prospecting for gold. First, I must take the time to work at it. Second, I must possess skills to do it effectively. Third, I need the patience to accept that much of my listening will bear little result. Fourth, I must recognize a nugget when I see it and know what to do with it.

> A good listener is not only popular everywhere, but after a while he gets to know something. — Wilson Mizner

---

Lord, keep me involved in discussions, which are an exchange of knowledge; but keep me from arguments, which are an exchange of ignorance.

As a manager, of course you want to encourage discussion and discourage argument. But how? No formula exists to accomplish this, but the following guidelines will help:

1. **Lead the listener to your point of view.** Don't push and shove. Nothing triggers an argument faster than an unexpected idea, an unwelcome order, or an abrupt transition.

2. **Don't exaggerate. Keep the issue within bounds.** In a reorganization situation, for example, tell exactly what

the change will mean. Don't make it sound as if the whole place will be turned upside down. Fear generates arguments.

3. **Tell the whole story.** If you don't, you will lose your credibility and no one will believe you the next time—a circumstance ripe for argument.

4. **Accent the positive.** Do this for obvious reasons, but don't sugarcoat.

5. **Give your people their say.** Besides cementing your rapport with employees, free discussion acts as a safety valve. Ask for their opinions, comments, and suggestions—but not merely to placate them. Give their ideas serious consideration.

6. **Itemize the message.** If necessary, give it in small pieces so people can understand it readily. Misunderstanding leads to arguments, so the purpose here is to minimize the chance for it.

7. **Backtrack if necessary.** Do this to determine if you are getting across, winning full understanding.

8. **Develop a network for feedback.** Probe as casually as possible with your most deliberate employees to test how well you are understood. If you aren't getting across well, repeat to minimize future arguments or misunderstanding.

9. **Keep calm.** Never show exasperation when you aren't getting across to others. Never accuse or threaten.

10. **Restudy your position when you meet persistent resistance.** Perhaps your stand has weak spots you overlooked. If you can find them, fix them.

> A gentle answer turns away wrath, but a harsh word stirs up anger.
> — Proverbs 15:1

Lord, never let me forget to explain why, as well as what, when I give an order.

When we order employees to do something, we must remember also to tell them why. If we fail, we are caught in the busy person's trap: Giving orders without explanation because it seems like the quickest and easiest way to get things done. Explaining may be the longest and hardest way, but in the long run it is the most efficient way.

Explanations provide these benefits:

- They show the logic and reasonableness of the order.

- They turn a command into a request.

- They lessen the chance of mistakes because people who understand why they are doing something are less likely to err.

- They make employees aware of the conditions surrounding the order so they are more likely to stop and ask for further clarification if the conditions change.

- They compliment employees by making them partners, not merely subordinates.

- They encourage suggestions, even when the reasons seem so obvious as scarcely to be worth mentioning.

Crises may occur when time seems too short for explanations. But even in most emergencies, we are unwise if we fail to find time for explanations.

> The plans of the diligent lead to profit as surely as haste leads to poverty.
> — Proverbs 21:5

> Do you see a man who speaks in haste? There is more hope for a fool than for him.
> — Proverbs 29:20

Lord, help me play a few perfect games.

Perfect games are possible, but not probable. For example, only two hundred no-hit games have been pitched in baseball's major leagues. But pitching a no-hitter is always the goal, because the fewer the hits, the fewer the chances of fielding errors and having runs scored against your team.

Just as the best defense against homeruns is not to allow any hits, the best defense against complaints is to prevent them. How? Let's look at four suggestions:

1. **Diagnose potential difficulties and trouble spots before they grow serious.** This is easier said than done, but it essentially involves alertness and being on top of your job.

2. **Guard your credibility.** If you are consistently fair, courteous, and patient, lack of credibility will not be a problem. Employees in a unit where the grievance record was remarkably low were interviewed to reveal the secret. One employee explained, "The boss is so decent you feel like a heel if you complain." Credibility is hard to develop, but *so* easy to lose.

3. **Give the full story.** On developments that affect your people, communicate the smallest details. Something that seems insignificant to you may be the key issue to others.

4. **Give advance notice.** Make a rule always to tell your people about everything that is coming up. And do it as far in advance as possible.

No major league pitcher has ever struck out twenty-seven batters in a regulation game. Neither will you ever pitch a "no-complaint" game. Nor should you necessarily believe you have reached perfection if you receive no complaints. You have more likely achieved totalitarianism, with no one brave enough to complain.

Perfection would come if we could follow completely Jesus' greatest commandment. No one since Christ has achieved that level of perfection, but he says we should keep trying.

> Love the Lord your God with all your heart and with all your soul and with all your mind. . . . And love your neighbor as yourself.
> — Matthew 22:37, 39

COMPENSATION

Lord, cause me to give as much attention to the compensation of each employee as I do to compensation for executives.

Corporations should have a compensation program for all its employees that follows the same principles the company follows for its executives. Underlying the executive program are a number of concepts. Some affect all forms of compensation; others relate only to specific types of pay or common-design approaches.

First, compensation should be hierarchical; at each

successively higher level, the total pay opportunity should increase. Executive compensation plans provide a means of achieving a more hierarchical pay structure because they restrict eligibility to executives at certain salary or title levels. The use of several plans can create a "tiered" approach to compensation, motivating individuals to progress in the organization so they win salary increases and become eligible for extra rewards.

Second, executive pay should vary with performance in a given year and over time—and do so more sharply than is possible through salaries alone. Incentive bonuses and executive stock plans, which match reward with performance, accomplish this.

Third, at successively higher levels of responsibility, more of the executive's total reward should be at risk. This concept affects the design and award patterns of most plans, increasing the size of the target bonus or stock award at each higher level and thereby reinforcing the hierarchical concept of pay.

Fourth, professional managers have a proprietary stake in the business, and their interest should be aligned directly with those of the stockholder. This concept provides one of the principal rationales for the adoption of an executive stock plan.

Fifth, an executive's compensation should facilitate the building of personal net worth. This concept helps explain the prevalence of executive stock plans and deferred compensation plans that provide opportunities for capital accumulation.

Sixth, the compensation vehicles used by the company should be cost effective in a way that has the least impact on company earnings. They should take advantage of those provisions of the law that enable corporations to provide tax-free or tax-favored compensation—thus delivering more net after-tax reward for every dollar of compensation expenditure; hence, the popularity of certain forms of executive stock options and perquisites.

Seventh, compensation plans should be used to retain key executives. This has led to the development of plans that make realizations of gains or payouts contingent on the recipient's continued employment.

Eight, because of their position, executives have unique needs that the company should help them meet to spare them concern about personal affairs and free them for company matters.

Ninth, executive compensation needs to be competitive both in the level of total reward and in the types of plans available.

Lord, help me remember these principles and use them in compensating all employees, not just executives.

COMPLAINTS

Lord, help me field complaints well to win the game.

Complaints are like fly balls, line drives, and grounders in a baseball game: they must be fielded by you and your fielding teammates. If you let a tough one get by you, the challenge becomes increasingly difficult.

The same is true for unfielded complaints, so take them in stride, but be aggressive in fielding them. Remember, the ball won't always be hit directly to you.

Expect complaints from three principal sources:

1. **From your boss.** Learn to differentiate between the serious and the trivial. A common mistake is to give undue weight to the superior's off-hand comments.

2. **From outside.** Most outside complaints are from customers and probably will be relayed to you through your boss. Treat them in the same way you would a grievance from your superior. Deal with all of them seriously and promptly, of course.

3. **From employees.** Most grievances you receive will come from your own people. If your plant is organized, your labor contract probably has an established procedure for dealing with them. We won't go into that because the mechanics vary, and the important point is not the mechanics; it's the communication and attitudes necessary to deal effectively with grievances. Facing up to problems that may have been wholly or partly of your making requires honesty and integrity.

The complaint openly presented rarely gives much trouble. But the grievance you don't know about or refuse to acknowledge causes a real headache. To sense something is wrong even though no one tells you about it directly requires a well-developed sense of perception. And psychological skill and courage are necessary to determine whether the apparent complaint is the real one.

Another problem is the repetitive complaint, but from a new grievant. Treat the complaint even more carefully than the first time you heard it, because there is almost certainly something wrong if it surfaces two or more times.

Here is what you can do about complaints:

1. **Listen objectively and imaginatively.**

2. **Investigate all charges.** Don't neglect those that seem trivial.

3. **Promise remedy if the grievant is right.** Be sure, however, that you tackle the real problem. Sometimes complaints lie within complaints. Grievances about odor, room temperature, and the like often camouflage the real complaint, possibly about your managerial style.

4. **Hold firm if no remedy is justified.** Show how you investigated the charge. Tactfully point out the grievant's erroneous facts or conclusions. This is particularly important in dealing with the chronic griper.

5. **Follow through.** Here is where the fielding often breaks down. No matter how well we stop the ball, if we don't make a good throw to the baseman we don't get an out, and the complaint is not resolved.

Aim for perfection. . . . — 2 Corinthians 13:11

CONFLICT OF INTEREST

Lord, give me wisdom to forestall conflicts before they happen, especially conflicts of interest.

> Trust in the Lord with all your heart
>   and lean not on your own understanding;
> in all your ways acknowledge him,
>   and he will make your paths straight.
> — Proverbs 3:5–6

After college, Wade joined the sales promotion department of a cosmetic firm. He worked there a year before he even faintly suspected that his boss had flexible ethics.

The suspicion was born at a Christmas party in his manager's swank Manhattan apartment where Wade saw on the walls the artwork for the firm's recent advertising campaign—all expensive original paintings by well-known artists. The suspicion reached adolescence shortly afterward. The boss's secretary had been out ill, and Wade took a call for her from the accounting department asking about a bill from Promotion Consultants, Inc. He found the firm's file, but it clarified nothing. He asked the manager.

"Oh that." He looked quickly at Wade. "I'll handle it."

"What is Promotion Consultants?" Wade asked.

"I use them for sales ideas," said the boss offhandedly. Yet Wade had never seen any representatives from Promotion Consultants in the office and knew nothing about what the firm contributed. Because the organization was near the office, he investigated during a lunch hour. Its name appeared on the lobby directory of a seedy Manhattan building. Wade took the rickety elevator to the fourth floor. At room 410, four names straggled down the frosted glass panel of the door, including an accountant; Promotion Consultors, Inc.; Creative Printing, Inc.; and American Advertising Specialties. Except for the accountant, Wade recognized them all from files he had seen while hunting for Promotion Consultors.

At his knock, the door opened a crack, to reveal part of a woman's elaborate hairdo and a right eye.

"How do you do," said Wade, summoning his most boyish grin. "I'm looking for someone from Promotion Consultors."

"They're out to lunch," said the woman in a husky voice.

"I'm wondering if they could help me on a product idea."

"They're quite busy now—all the work they can handle."

"Well, I can find someone else—in the *Yellow Pages*."

"Is that where you found us, in the *Yellow Pages?*"

"Ah . . . yes."

Wade turned and left for the elevator. He recognized the bee-hive hairdo and the husky voice as belonging to a woman he had met at the boss's Christmas party. And he had an uneasy feeling that he would not find Promotion Consultors listed in the *Yellow Pages*. He chided himself for not checking beforehand.

As he feared, the *Yellow Pages* did not list Promotion Consultors, nor Creative Printing, nor American Advertising Specialties, nor A. H. Smith, the accountant named on the door panel. He found them all, however, in the white-page directory, with different phone numbers but the same addresses.

Wade turned suspicion into certainty when he called the accounting department and asked for the latest endorsed checks paid to the three firms—giving as an excuse the possibility of a payment mixup. The three checks had been negotiated through different banks, but they were endorsed by A. H. Smith, A. Haring Smith and Arlette H. Smith, respectively. He couldn't remember the name of the husky-voiced woman he had met at the Christmas party, but he suspected it had been Arlette Smith.

Although Wade was now certain that his boss dealt with at least three dummy firms, he didn't know what to do about it. For a while he did nothing except tell his fiancee. She urged caution.

The situation bothered him, and he investigated further. He learned that Arlette Smith was indeed an accountant. She was unmarried. And another piece fell in place when he learned she had an apartment in the same building as his boss. The key piece turned up when Wade learned that Arlette and his manager had worked together for another cosmetic firm years ago.

Still, Wade did nothing. One day the boss called him into his office. "Wade, I notice from your vacation request that you want to take it this year in April."

"Yes, I'm getting married. Honeymoon."

"Congratulations!" The manager got up and shook his hand vigorously. "Wade, I have a suggestion. We need to research our French perfume competitors. Learn the latest sales promotion gimmicks they're using. How would you like to go to Paris, look into things? And of course take your honeymoon at the same time." The boss paused. "We might even pick up your wife's tab."

"Gosh, that sounds wonderful, sir. We had planned Bermuda." Wade didn't expect this. "I'll ask my fiancee."

That night he talked with her. She remained unusually quiet, saying only, "Gosh, Wade, it makes me feel kind of funny."

"If I accepted, it would put me into a conflict-of-interest situation," Wade mused. Then he added, "Not to mention what's pretty close to a bribe. Something tells me he's bought off other people around the place with deals like he's offering me. His secretary dresses like a high-fashion model. How can she afford it?"

His fiancee said, "Paris would be nice in April."

"I don't feel right about it."

"What's so wrong?"

"It's not right. My conscience would bother me."

For the rest of the evening, by unspoken mutual consent, they talked of other things. When he left, she obliquely returned to the pressing issue. "Sometimes it's best to handle conflict by avoiding it."

"You mean, go along with this for now and take a stand another day when the issues are more clearcut?"

"Something like that."

"Honey, the issue here is as clearcut as it will ever be. I've got to resolve this now, or it will eat me up."

"Who says so?"

He considered for a moment, then replied, "God says so."

The next day, Wade called the company's president from a pay phone. He got an appointment for later that morning.

The president listened without saying a word as Wade told the story, showed him copies of the dummy companies' bills, the peculiar listings in the telephone directory, and the check endorsements with the name variations and identical handwriting.

The president gazed thoughtfully out the window. "This will have to be investigated even more thoroughly than you already have done. That'll take time." He paused. "But we don't want him to fly the coop. When you go back to your office after lunch, see him and accept that Paris trip. Let him think he's bought you."

Wade shifted at a sudden thought. "But sir, what if he goes ahead and makes reservations, buys airline tickets for Paris?"

"So much the better. We'll have that much more on him." The president smiled for the first time. "You may even take that sales-promotion-cum-honeymoon trip to France—at my expense."

Wade and his bride did honeymoon in Paris. Wade even did a little sales promotion study for the firm. The suspected fraud investigation turned up far more than anyone had suspected. Besides receiving payment for nonexistent work supposedly performed for the cosmetic firm, the three dummy companies also served as the funnel through which the manager had been receiving kickbacks from legitimate printers, ad agencies, and other vendors. The ex-boss, his secretary, and Arlette had embezzled nearly a million dollars over nine years.

CONFORMITY

Lord, make me think things out afresh and never

blindly accept conventional ideas and ways of doing things.

Convention can grip us with iron almost from birth. Our parents teach us early what is "proper." Teachers impart to us wisdom, usually conventional. Friends and associates in our adult life convey what is "right," although not always by example. Worst of all, we build personal conventions of beliefs, habits, and thought processes that become almost sacred to us.

Today's managers face a critical dilemma that is related to our dependency on conventional thinking. Suppose a bright young person working for you asks about prospects for a promotion. With the aftereffects of the recession still being felt and with demands for leaner management ranks and increased productivity, there are not enough promotions available above entry-level management jobs to meet the demand from qualified employees. So you can't honestly say, as managers could in the 1950s and 60s, "Be patient, your turn will come soon."

How do you counsel now, trying to be hopeful, not to sound patronizing, and to keep the young employee contented—all at the same time?

You can't make promises about the future if you are not sure the promotion freeze will be lifted. Promises about something happening "down the road" may be well-intended, but they are too vague and open-ended to make much difference.

Nor will simple pats on the back help. "We think highly of you" can satisfy only a few times without concrete evidence, such as a salary boost and/or promotion, to back it up.

But you can give less conventional rewards to a good

performer, aside from pay boosts and upgrades. For example:

- Assign new responsibilities to the employee to make the job more challenging. If you do this, however, be sure to relieve him or her of some old assignments. If practical, let the person pick the ones to shed. The ambitious employee wants challenges.

- Enroll the employee in a seminar or course, particularly something involving new technologies or new managerial methods. Energetic people welcome new learning experiences.

- Encourage the employee to take business trips. (Now and then you might even pick up the expense for a spouse). Although salary budgets are tight, lids on education and travel probably aren't so heavy.

- "Volunteer" the ambitious employee for a government committee or even detached, although limited, service.

- As a last resort, transfer the individual to another department. Your main aim is to keep the talented person, but sometimes that is possible only elsewhere in the company. Then at least you have the hope of getting him or her back later.

Above all, communicate to the frustrated, valued employee your sympathy and your willingness to help.

> We are most likely to get angry and excited in our opposition to some idea when we ourselves are not quite certain of our own position, and are inwardly tempted to take the other side. — Thomas Mann, Buddenbrooks

Nothing is more dangerous than an idea, when it's the only one we have.
— Alain [Emile Chartier], Systeme des Beaux-Arts

CONTROL

Lord, keep me in control of my operation, lest it control me.

One of the most difficult challenges for a manager is maintaining control of fast-acting situations that occur simultaneously. For example, a sudden sharp rise in sales resulted in lower, not higher profits for my company because the phenomenon strained normal controls in our accounting, inventory, marketing, and payroll departments. Here's how it happened.

In his haste to rush orders, my accounting manager "temporarily" ignored his controls, discovering after it was too late that we did some of the added business at a loss. A particularly strong personality running inventory control, a squeaking wheel whom no one wanted to hear, kept stock levels too low. In the euphoria of rising sales my marketing control man "forgot" that we were taking too many small orders at which our profit margins were too low. Payroll controls went awry because we added permanent people when we should have taken temporaries.

I mistakenly assumed that the people responsible for each area would act in concert with one another. To guarantee that that would happen I should have installed proper controls at monthly milestones instead of quarterly. I should have monitored cooperation among the four control managers. I would have tailored the controls for the unexpected (and temporary, as it developed) rise in sales. In short, the tailor should have had more sense.

CREATIVITY

Lord, keep reminding me that "the way we've always done things" is not necessarily the best way to do them.

The whole trend of Western European-American society is toward ends based on these assumptions:

1. The expenditure of physical and mental effort is natural and will be as readily expended at work as at play.
2. Control and the threat of punishment are not the only means of getting people to do things.
3. Commitment to objectives is as strong a motivating force as the expectation of rewards for achievement.
4. Under proper conditions, the average person seeks and accepts responsibility. When he or she does not, such behavior results from bad experience, not an inherent human characteristic.
5. Creativity is widely, not narrowly, distributed among human beings.
6. Human capabilities are only partly utilized.

We see this trend realized in freer attitudes toward children, the altered husband-wife relationship, the improving status of minority groups. Democracy itself has its foundations on these six assumptions.

In contrast, the traditional authoritarian approach still holds sway ideologically over many governments of the world and some businesses. It rests on three other implicit assumptions about human nature: (a) that most people dislike work and will avoid it if possible; (b) that most people must be coerced into working because they dislike effort intensely; (c) that most people like to be directed and dislike leading.

Many American businessmen find themselves in a transitional state today—partly following permissive practices, partly holding to some authoritarian vestiges. The pyramidal organizational structure can readily promote authoritarianism because it encourages top-down rule. Yet, it largely persists because business, government, the military, and the church "have always been" organized that way. Old habits die hard.

Yet even within the pyramid of organizational structure we can see remarkable diversity. Some examples, among many:

- Flexible employee benefits and working hours, once considered bizarre, are increasingly common.

- Thanks to the computer, more and more companies allow employees to work full- or part-time at home.

- Temporary task forces, work groups, and other ad hoc organizational setups flourish within the conventional pyramid.

Why? To accommodate diversity. God made each person unique, and managers who are able to manage employees according to their individual strengths or weaknesses will be much more successful in motivating them than a manager who, for lack of imagination or under the guise of "being fair," treats everyone alike.

Lord, give me sincerity, the essence of originality.

One definition of sincerity is honest genuineness, the ability to acknowledge seemingly alien facts and ideas.

Answer the following questions to get an idea of your own creativity quotient:

1. Can you get enthusiastic about problems outside your specialized area?
2. Do you feel excited and challenged in solving major or minor problems in many areas?
3. When a problem at first seems uninteresting, do you persist with it, anticipating that it will become interesting?
4. Do you understand what is expected of you by management?
5. Do you seldom assume limitations in your work?
6. Do you recognize weakening persistence for what it is and set the problem aside temporarily, to return to it another day?
7. Do you resist "blocking" a project, even though you think it trivial and distracting from problems more to your taste?
8. Do you occasionally accept illogical thoughts from your subconscious mind, recognizing that they can help creativity?
9. Do you carry a notebook in which to record ideas?
10. Do you seek many ideas, not settling for a few?
11. Can you simplify and organize your impressions?

If you honestly answered yes to eight of the eleven questions, your creativity level is high.

Creative people need great tenacity of purpose and stubborn resistance to discouragment. They need to accept a partnership of their subconscious and conscious minds. They need initiative, curiosity, and the ability to simplify the myriad impressions that descend on them. Above all, they need a firm belief in the validity of their ideas.

Highly talented researchers had given up trying to find a way to frost electric light bulbs on the inside. The challenge had degenerated into a kind of joke whereby every embryonic engineer was given the "impossible" assignment. Veterans at General Electric put Marvin Pipkin, a new engineer, through the usual routine. All were either amused or mildly conscience-stricken when Pipkin assumed they were sincere and took the problem seriously. But their amusement and guilt changed to total surprise when he actually discovered a way to frost bulbs on the inside. He also found a way to etch the glass with soft, rounded pits for added strength and maximum diffusion of light.

> The merit of originality is not novelty; it is sincerity. The believing man is the original man; whatsoever he believes, he believes it for himself, not for another. — Thomas Carlyle

---

Lord, guide me toward true self-confidence, a fundamental of creativity.

A lack of true self-confidence turns up frequently in people with a high potential for creativity. We tend to assume gifted people recognize their ability and, therefore, act confidently; but often they do not. Perhaps they dimly realize their high potential and unconsciously fear it will not be fulfilled.

Sometimes people with creative potential lack social graces or athletic skills. This may cause them embarrassment and loss of self-confidence, particularly in youth when they tend to exaggerate imagined failures.

Occasionally, a real failure jolts a creative person to such an extent that he or she loses both self-confidence and creativity.

The inability to find the right niche often discourages potentially creative people into resignation—eventually they accept the role of being a square peg in a round hole, at the sacrifice of innovative capabilities.

The niche-finding problem particularly afflicts business people, and the failure to solve it undoubtedly smothers many creative business careers.

Besides finding the right spot and circumstances, take these steps to gain self-confidence:

1. Get experience because creativity thrives on it.

2. Watch out for dead-end jobs, if only because they tend to stifle innovative potential.

3. Act enthusiastically because that will help give you real enthusiasm, which always aids creativity.

4. Put your failures in proper perspective; remember, creative people generally experience more failures than those who are non-creative because they try more things and take more chances.

5. Recognize your weaknesses and either strengthen them or offset them so they won't inhibit your productivity of ideas.

6. Show courage above all; you need it for creativity.

7. Give your best. Unconfident people seldom exert themselves to the fullest, perhaps because they fear to

discover that their best may seem none too good. Yet, the very nature of creativity involves reaching beyond where anybody has reached before. You can never achieve anything new without stretching.

Note, however, that we emphasize developing *true* self-confidence, not conceit.

Lord, grant me a poor memory so I can forget preconceived ideas that stifle creativity.

Children possess candor because they are not inhibited by years of experience, training, or knowledge about what is "commonly known." As a result, they are capable of perceptive insights, creative analogies, and astonishing visions often denied to those of us who are older and more inhibited.

The ability to forget, at the right moments, what we know is a requirement of originality. If we cannot forget, we clutter our minds with obvious answers that never allow original ideas a chance to develop.

Thomas Edison carried the art of forgetting to such extremes that on one occasion, when he was standing in line to pay taxes at New York City Hall, he forgot his name when the clerk called it.

The absent-minded professor or scientist is a stock figure we poke fun at, but these people know how to forget when they are trying to find the answer to a question or problem.

If we are not children, how can we deliberately summon childlike candor? Here are some suggestions:

Visualize in wordless images. Let your subconscious mind anesthetize your conscious and restore the innocence of vision. Practice thinking in terms of pictures, not words. Andrew Higgins, a New Orleans boat builder during World War II, did so. He and others in his business were asked by the government to develop a vehicle or craft suitable for landing troops on beaches. A native of Louisiana, he visualized the shallow-draft swamp and bayou boats used in his state. His mind also saw the big trucks delivering goods for ships docked at New Orleans wharves. He combined the two images and the result was a specialized amphibious landing craft used in the Pacific and European theaters during World War II.

Shift the emphasis. Our subconscious minds do this more easily than our conscious minds, but we can spur the subconscious along such lines by deliberately giving our conscious minds practice in shifting emphasis. Our subconscious will follow. For exercise, pick a problem. Do you have trouble with job-hopping secretaries? Think of hiring older women instead of recent secretarial school graduates. Are you short of warehousing space? Think of your rail or truck transport service as a warehouse, which would allow deliveries to be scheduled more closely to jibe with production needs.

Use analogy. Again, practicing with the conscious mind helps exercise the skill of the subconscious. Look for analogies. Is there an analogy between what you do to improve quality control on the job and what you do to improve the quality of your child's schoolwork? What analogies can you see between the design of children's toys and the design of your own products?

Impersonate. Put yourself in another's place. Imagine how you would act as the department manager. As a doctor. As a salesman trying to sell something. This is one of the most common ways of forgetting; it happens frequently in dreams.

Symbolize and make concrete. William Harvey, an English physician and anatomist, watched the exposed heart valve at work in a living fish and suddenly visualized it as a pump—a conception that led to his vital seventeenth-century discovery of how blood circulates. In dreams, we commonly symbolize. Thinking in symbols becomes a form of forgetting or a way of imagining in uncommon patterns. The trick is to transform the symbols into specific or material things that will help us get valid ideas or transform abstractions into concrete terms.

The Bible abounds in symbols—the shepherd and his flock, seeds and other agricultural images, the rock—that convert abstract concepts such as responsibility, growth, and stability into everyday things around us.

Lord, spare me from mediocrity, even though it is the ascendent power among mankind.

The great danger of mediocrity is not that it is so prevalent, but that so many people parade as creative, exceptional individuals when they are not. They fool many of us and—much worse—even themselves.

Almost everyone wants to be creative, and everyone can develop that attribute. But the striving for the creative image has sometimes led to the creative facade. When we have only the image but not the substance, we have trouble.

One of the problems with on-the-job creativity is that much of the activity that passes as creative is not. For example, do you recognize these people?

- Those who talk the creative game, frequently using variations of the word and its synonyms in conversation.

- Those who exhibit the trappings of creativity by displaying one of the more discreet bits of pop art in their office, wearing the latest fashion in dress, and using the latest buzz-words in conversation.

- Those who like group activities and meetings. They are always ready to brainstorm for creative ideas but don't really know what brainstorming procedures truly involve.

- Those who say they want creative ideas from subordinates, but find flaws in nearly all of them.

- Those who really don't know creativity when they see it, mistaking it for mere flair, knack, workmanship, or imitation, or confusing it with bright but irrelevant and superficial ideas.

The last trait—not knowing what the exceptional, creative action really is—is the most serious flaw.

We call many people "creative" when actually they just have a flair or a knack. We do not downgrade aptitude because it is necessary and valuable; yet, if we mistake it for genuine creativity, we may stop unnecessarily short of true innovation.

A hobbyist whose vase designs copy her evening school teacher's may have a knack, but she does not become creative until she makes vases of her own design. A writer of social criticism may comment perceptively and cleverly, but he doesn't become creative until he offers constructive suggestions on how to remedy our ills.

Most creative people also have a flair, but the reverse doesn't always apply. And occasionally a creative person may not even show much apparent aptitude for the field in which he or she eventually displays marked innovative gifts. For instance, Paul Winchell, a ventriloquist by profession, holds several patents of value to industry.

Good workmanship by itself does not necessarily constitute creativity, just as a knack does not always equate with innovation. Again, we do not downgrade workmanship, but we urge that you not mistake it for creativity.

Administrators of suggestion systems have long been familiar with a phenomenon—the most prolific idea submitters seldom are the best workmen. The specialization inherent in good workmanship apparently tends to dull the creative abilities. This often happens because specialization may make the work an end in itself and because it may put psychological blinders on people.

Exceptional people often shine in many fields. Geoffrey Chaucer, author of *Canterbury Tales,* performed as a skilled diplomat and helped to establish the beginnings of Britain's customs system. Anthony Trollope, the nineteenth century English novelist, is also the father of Great Britain's modern postal system. Benjamin Franklin was a printer, journalist, pamphleteer, politician, wire-puller, diplomat, statesman, and the first U. S. postmaster-general, pioneer of electricity, founder of the physics of liquid surfaces, discoverer of the properties of marsh gas, designer of the *chevaux de frise* which halted the advance of the British fleet on the Delaware, inventor of bifocal spectacles and of improved fireplaces and stoves, advocate of watertight bulkheads on ships and of chimneyshafts for the ventilation of mines.

Contemporary examples seem to be proportionately fewer than those from former times. Perhaps the unprecedented expansion in our total body of knowledge compels us to specialize, thus limiting our range and creative potential.

Stealing, imitating, or combining the ideas of others do not constitute creativity, yet they sometimes parade as creativity.

Real creativity demands relevance. For example, proponents of electric cars have periodically promoted the auto since early in this century. Yet, the idea has never taken off because the car has too many drawbacks: it can't take off at high speeds, it requires heavy batteries, and it can't perform adequately in hilly terrain.

Creation may be miraculously effortless or agonizing. Yet, quick or slow, watch out for the superficial idea—the lightweight notions that have only expediency or a transitory gloss to recommend them.

In the fourth week of a bitter strike, a manufacturer put all its management on half-salary for the duration—a cost-cutting measure with guaranteed effectiveness. The side effects, however, proved disastrous. Ten percent quit on the spot, another fifteen percent left within a year. The expense of recruiting one-fourth of a new managerial staff far outweighed the money saved by the diminished salaries. In addition, the damage done to the morale of remaining managers could never be measured.

Some individuals wrongly describe themselves or others as uncreative or mediocre, either because they produce so few ideas or because they take so long to develop those they have. Take heart. If you assign one hundred as an index for a fully creative person—such as Da Vinci or Franklin—the individual with average creativity might have an index of seven or eight. Even ten is better than average. Most of us have wide capabilities of moving from mediocre to exceptional levels.

God gave all of us the potential for creativity.

CREDIBILITY

Lord, help me give credit where it is due or, if there is doubt, even where it is not fully due.

Kevin was the only person in the audience who neither laughed nor smiled when his boss ended his acceptance speech for the company's man-of-the-year award by saying he was "tops in humility."

Kevin believed his boss had stolen the award from him. The man had claimed credit for more than a score of cost-saving ideas that had originated with Kevin. But what could a mere employee do?

For a time Kevin just smoldered, not wanting to air the issue in public. He considered quitting, but he finally decided on a different approach. In private, he confronted his boss.

"I was disappointed that you didn't give me a little of the credit in your acceptance speech."

The manager held out his hands palms upward. "Kev, I did. I said the whole thing was a group effort."

"If I'm a group, that's right. But I'm a person. I didn't hear my name mentioned once.

"Kev, I can see you're upset, and I'm sorry. But I

couldn't name just you. Then the rest of the gang would be upset."

"I don't see why." Kevin hunched forward. "They had nothing to do with any of the ideas that won you the award."

His boss edged forward. "Wait a minute! You're accusing me of credit hogging. This whole thing was a group deal. Sure, you had the lead role in it, but it was a team effort. And I said so at the podium."

They parted with the issue unresolved and with each sincerely believing he had been maligned.

Over time, many sharp edges of truth change subtly in the view of the beholder, and in this case neither Kevin nor his manager were seeing the landscape clearly. It was true that Kevin had assumed the lead role, as the manager acknowledged. It was also true that the other people in the group had all made contributions; but none of them had been major. If the manager had cited anyone in his acceptance talk, he should have mentioned Kevin. The manager thought, mistakenly, that he had bypassed trouble by not naming anyone.

Kevin's case teaches us several lessons:

1. **Be generous in giving credit to others.** If there is a question of how much credit is due, it is better to give too much than not enough. Although Kevin's manager erred in this regard, Kevin had brought some of the trouble on himself. He had always been a loner, never cooperating well in group projects, always jealous of his supposed rights. The manager didn't mention his name out of spite as well as stupidity. It would have cost him nothing to have mentioned Kevin's name. The boss would have gained a loyal and gifted ally if he had suggested Kevin as the man-of-the-year winner in his

stead. A manager reaps real rewards in having gifted people work for him because they ease his job and contribute to his success.

Vanity eventually impelled Kevin, introverted and normally inarticulate, to take his case to the company's president. Although the president's discreet investigation did not support Kevin completely, it did reveal that he had imaginative cost-cutting talents that the company didn't fully use. Kevin soon won a lateral transfer to a component where the president believed his abilities would find better use. His former manager didn't lose his job or his man-of-the-year award, but he never won another plaque, nor did he ever get promoted again.

2. **Never steal credit yourself.** In taking undue credit you establish your reputation as a thief, a disastrous blotch on your reputation that you may never be able to erase. You also run the risk of making yourself look ridiculous. A classic case occurred in an early movie version of *The Taming of the Shrew*. The credits read, "By William Shakespeare, with additional dialogue by Sam Taylor."

3. **Know your colleagues**—including your employees and your boss. Let's face it, some people are unscrupulous. Know who might try to steal credit and take *reasonable* precautions. You can relax if you adopt a few common-sense practices.

First, sign your work. You can do this easily if you must write reports, memos, or letters about it. Sometimes it pays to prepare such a document to be certain you stake your claim, even if it serves no other purpose.

Second, let discreet people know, in general terms, what you are doing. Many people think of secrecy as the ultimate precaution. Yet booby traps lie everywhere. In a work environment it is difficult, perhaps impossible, to maintain full secrecy. Just trying to keep something secret is a challenge for some people to try to unmask the mystery. Secrecy might also alienate you from many of your fellow employees. It's far more effective to speak freely about your project in general but to say little about it in particular.

The ultimate safeguard is trust. If you are generous in giving credit to others, if you never usurp credit yourself, and if you are a genuine friend of your employees and associates, most will return the favor.

> In everything, do to others what you would have them do to you.
> — Matthew 7:12

Lord, give me the tact to make a point without making an enemy.

General Electric had a Swedish supervisor in its Lamp Division who was a whiz as a teacher because he knew how to make an effective point.

In his office he had pictures of old equipment. "That shows how the shop looked in 1936," he would explain to someone in for a coffee break. "Our average pay was fifty cents an hour and you could hardly see the fringe benefits, so small they were. It's better now, don't you think?"

He could also make a point without uttering a word. He would stand and silently watch someone at work. If the employee glanced his way somewhat nervously, he would smile and nod. In so doing, he expressed approval, and he reinforced the person's attitudes toward work.

If he had to grant no pay increase or a very small one, he would say, "I think I know our trouble; I did not boss you good enough. Let's do better from now on."

The Swede could listen well, too, and make effective points that way. "Goot, goot," he would exclaim at something an employee said or did. "I remember dat," and he would because he was an inveterate note taker. Days, weeks, or even months later, he would take some action or make some remark that showed he had listened or watched and remembered. Yet, if he disagreed with some comment, he would smile sadly, touch the speaker and say, "I wish I heard you better." When someone offered an idea that especially delighted him, he would invite others to hear the originator repeat the pearl of wisdom.

If someone talked too much, the Swede could sometimes halt the speaker in mid-sentence by saying, "I watched you talking; now I want to watch you hearing."

Once the Swede was trying to get an employee to perform his job in a different way. "All right," the employee said at last, "I'll do it for your sake." But the Swede interrupted. "Never do it for my sake. Do it for your own. This benefits you. Try it, you'll like it." He knew not to use personal affection or esteem to make a point because that is a subtle form of bribery.

When the Swede was asked why he selected a job candidate who looked slower and more deliberate than another, he explained, "If I have to choose between a man who looks fast and a man who looks slow, I lean toward the slow man. Experience tells me he's more likely to have character. Here, we need character most, the kind that won't wear out fast."

> Rebuke a wise man and he will love you. Instruct a wise man and he will be wiser still; teach a righteous man and he will add to his learning.
> — Proverbs 9:8–9

Lord, hold me to the truth, even in small things.

> A shepherd boy, not thinking much,
>   Gave false alarms of "Wolf!" and such,
> 'Til none came to his yelp
>   Of Help! Help! Help! Help!"
> When a real wolf put him in dutch.

The outright lie in the "cry wolf" story is relatively rare. More commonly, it's the "little things" that undermine credibility. These are the half-truths, the exaggerations, the seemingly deft side-steps of responsibility, and the evasions.

> Lord, who may dwell in your sanctuary?
>   Who may live on your holy hill?
> He whose walk is blameless
>   and who does what is righteous,
> who speaks the truth from his heart
>   and has no slander on his tongue,
> who does his neighbor no wrong
>   and casts no slur on his fellow man,
> who despises a vile man,
>   but honors those who fear the Lord,
> who keeps his oath. . . .
>
> He who does these things
>   will never be shaken.
> — Psalm 15

DECEIT

Lord, teach me to resist fraud in myself and detect it in others.

Here is what some wise people have said on this subject:

> Fraud and falsehood only dread examination. Truth invites it. — Thomas Cooper (1759–1851)

> The handwriting on the wall may be a forgery.
> — Ralph Hodgson

> Whatever is only almost true is quite false, and among the most dangerous of errors, because being so near truth, it is the more likely to lead astray.
> — Henry Ward Beecher (1813–1887)

> The fellow who never makes a mistake takes his orders from one who does. — Herbert V. Prochnow

> *As a matter of fact* is an expression that precedes many an expression that isn't. — Laurence J. Peter

> One may smile, and smile, and be a villain.
> — William Shakespeare (1564–1616)

> Food gained by fraud tastes sweet to a man, but he ends up with a mouth full of gravel. — Proverbs 20:17

DECISION-MAKING

Lord, give me the courage to make a decision because no decision may be worse than a wrong one.

Dwight stopped in the men's room before going to the vice president's office. He washed his hands to stop the sweating. He knew the vice president wanted to talk about "reorganization in accounting." Ever since the previous accounting manager had died unexpectedly three months earlier, the post had been vacant. The vice president had taken over, as "acting manager, not the permanent head of the department," he told the staff. Dwight's hopes for the position waned as the weeks went by.

His wife urged him to ask for the post outright, but he didn't like doing that. Then she suggested he hunt for another job. He had gone as far as writing a resume, but he had not yet sent it to anyone. Perhaps now the indecision his wife decried would prove to be the patience he claimed it was. He would get the job.

"Come in, come in," called the vice president as Dwight stood uncertainly in the doorway. Dwight started toward the chair before the officer's desk.

"No, no, let's both sit on the couch," said the vice president. In the shift of direction, the accountant barked his left shin against the edge of a coffee table in front of the couch. The pain caused him to miss the other's first words.

" . . . appreciate your patience in waiting us out for a decision on this reorganization," he was saying.

Dwight's spirits lifted and the pain subsided. "I wanted to give you time for consideration," the accountant said solemnly.

The vice president shot a quick look at the other, then gazed out the window, as though fascinated by the cloudy day outside. "Have you ever run across a fellow named Charles Heller?"

Dwight frowned anxiously. "No, I don't believe I have."

"He's an accountant, too, was with Consolidated."

"Was?"

"He's joining us as of the first of the month as manager of accounting." When Dwight said nothing, the vice president finished in a rush, "You'll be promoted to manager of accounting programs, reporting to Heller. Congratulations!"

"I had hoped to be named manager," Dwight finally said.

"But you never told me you wanted the job."

"Well, no, it didn't seem appropriate." Then, as often happens with diffident and normally inarticulate people, Dwight began to talk too much. All his frustrations poured out.

When he ran down, the other said, "I'm glad we talked. From what you've said, this new job will be right up your alley."

Dwight felt so drained that only a trace of bitterness crept into his question. "What will accounting programs involve?"

The officer looked judicious. "We have ideas, but I'd like you to discuss it with Heller. We welcome your views, too. As a new job, we'll be feeling our way. I have in mind a planning role for you." When Dwight looked blank, the vice president hurried on. "The promotion means more money—a hundred a month more."

When the interview ended, Dwight didn't know what to think.

When no forthright discussion occurs with a passed-over employee, the company, its management, and the

DECISION-MAKING 83

individual all lose. The following elements should be included in a frank talk:

1. The reasons for another choice. In the interview, the vice president never explained why he had picked Heller over Dwight. Instead, he pretended he was making two promotions. The officer's subterfuge was indecisiveness as serious as Dwight's.

2. An opportunity for the loser to express his or her side. Although the vice president should have sought and welcomed Dwight's reactions before he made his final decision, he didn't because he guessed they'd be unpleasant. Faced with a situation like this, many bosses are less than courageous and try to gloss over the situation. This is another form of indecision that may return to haunt the offender. On the other hand, the loser should take the initiative and insist on giving his views if not invited to do so. Dwight gave his, but in a chaotic, unpersuasive form—again the result of chronic indecision.

3. A discussion of the loser's future with the present employer. The vice president scarcely mentioned this in his vague description of Dwight's new job—another form of indecision by the officer. He should have been painstakingly explicit.

4. An offer to help the loser get another job. This might be with the same employer but in another department, or it could be with another company. Even if the vice president wanted Dwight to stay, he should have offered him his help in the shift if Dwight chose to leave. If the promotion had been genuine, he still should have made the relocation offer—with suitable disclaimers and with the frank explanation that he knew the loser had hoped for the higher job.

5. Suggestions concerning the loser's best career course. This is different from the offer to help get another job. Failure to win a hoped-for promotion nearly always damages a person's self-concept. At the least, reassurance is necessary because self-doubt normally rides hard on the heels of such a defeat. By implication, the vice president gave such reassurance in saying, by means of the promotion offer, "Stay with us. You may still have a satisfactory career." He should have stated this directly and with the new job's details.

Events proved the implication false. Dwight's new job as manager of accounting programs turned out to be the same as his old job. As the years passed and he stayed on, he became ill and had to retire on a disability pension. The vice president didn't last either. Heller took over in the next reorganization. Both Dwight and the vice president should have remembered Aesop's fable about why the bat grew blind:

> The poor bat could not make up his mind
> In caves he would wander
> The better to ponder,
> But he stayed there so long he grew blind.

Lord, grant me the judgment to balance the present and the future, with the knowledge that good decisions now make the future more manageable.

Quentin gave up his job selling mutual funds for a New York firm to take over his father's business as a manufacturers' representative for specialty steel products in New England.

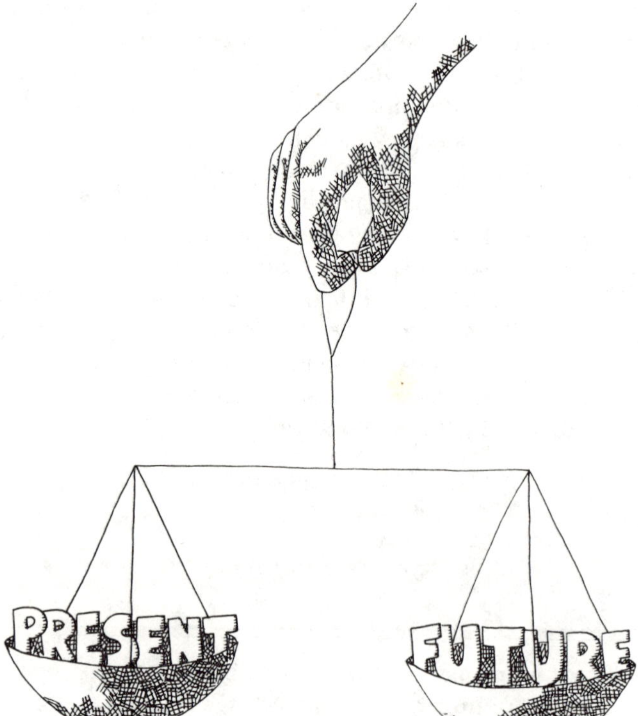
PRESENT
FUTURE

His father had long urged such a move, but Quentin had resisted, both because the business couldn't support two men and because he and his father didn't always get along well. Both were strong-willed and liked to have their own way. When the father finally promised to retire completely, however, Quentin agreed to take over his sales business.

The first danger signal sounded when Quentin's parents decided after a three months' trial that Florida didn't suit them as a place for retirement. They returned to Hartford, where Quentin and his wife had moved after purchasing the parents' home. The older couple moved into an apartment, but they made it clear they didn't approve of structural changes in the house, which Quentin had remodeled to permit him an office in his home.

"It's much better to have your office downtown in a prestigious building," grumbled his father. "And you can meet people for lunch easier."

"But I'm on the road three-fourths of the time, not in downtown Hartford," countered Quentin. "An office in the house maximizes my time with the family. And it saves money because Beth can act as a secretary when I'm out."

At first the father said nothing about the decline in volume under Quentin's management, even though it meant less income than he had expected from the modest override Quentin gave him as payment for the business. When no substantial improvement occurred after a year, the father complained.

"Dad, you know steel sales generally are down. We've got to grin and bear it."

But Dad could do neither and began making "suggestions." Soon father and son found themselves in near warfare. An irrelevant event triggered the final break. Quentin's mother criticized Beth's taste in redecorating the house. Quentin and his family returned to New York where he resumed selling mutual funds. The father left retirement with relief to take up his business again.

In an attempt to pave the way to the future, Quentin's Hartford sojourn proved a wasteful detour. In resuming his mutual funds sales, he had lost many customers in the fifteen months he had been away from that business. He incorrectly balanced the present and the future.

Yet career and job changes *do* work out. Although many books have been written on how to appraise a proposed change in your life, most suggestions boil down to these:

- Diagnose the situation to define basic problems and parameters, to clarify your objectives, and to identify a solution.

- Study the facts to isolate the key factors affecting your decision. A shorthand way to do this is to list all the pluses and minuses that you and your friends can think of concerning the decision.

- Develop alternative courses of action. Perhaps neither the status quo nor the change under consideration is right for you. Think of others.

- Evaluate each alternative to determine which one best meets your specific needs.

- Consider Proverbs 3:5–6:

> Trust in the Lord with all your heart. . . .
>   In all your ways acknowledge him,
> and he will make your paths straight.

Lord, teach me to look before I leap.

> There is a time for everything,
> and a season for every activity under heaven:
> > a time to be born and a time to die,
> > a time to plant and a time to uproot,
> > a time to kill and a time to heal,
> > a time to tear down and a time to build,
> > a time to weep and a time to laugh,
> > a time to mourn and a time to dance,
> > a time to scatter stones and a time to gather them,
> > a time to embrace and a time to refrain,
> > a time to search and a time to give up,
> > a time to keep and a time to throw away,
> > a time to tear and a time to mend,
> > a time to be silent and a time to speak,
> > a time to love and a time to hate,
> > a time for war and a time for peace.
>
> — Ecclesiastes 3:1–8

Absent from most of our lives today are periods of intellectual and spiritual pause for reflection. Engineering studies tell us that first-line managers do six hundred different things in an eight-hour day. May the Lord help us slow down so we may think and perform more effectively.

DELEGATION

Lord, help me learn to delegate.

Managers should never expect to run everything. And if they try, poor results are almost inevitable. However, the manager is still accountable.

There's the rub: How to balance direct accountability with indirect responsibility. The best way to juggle the two successfully is to clearly advise submanagers in which areas they can:

1. Act without advising or asking anyone.
2. Act but report to designated persons what they have done.
3. Act only if they have informed the manager in advance.
4. Act only after receiving instructions.

> Do not rule over them ruthlessly, but fear your God.
> — Leviticus 25:43

DISCIPLINE

Lord, teach me to use discipline as a tool, not as a weapon.

Webster defines discipline as "training which corrects, molds, strengthens, or perfects." A secondary definition is "punishment, chastisement." Many people, however, consider the secondary meaning as the most important or even the only definition.

Here are some suggestions for using discipline positively:

Treat people as if they are what they ought to be. This is the best way to help them become what they are capable of being. People usually act as we expect them to act. If we expect them to want to work, to accept commitments and responsibility, to wish to develop their creativity and other capabilities, most of them will. On the other hand, if we treat them as though we anticipate goldbricking and slack performance, that's probably what we'll get. The point: Don't expect bad actions; expect good behavior. Most people want to do right voluntarily.

Demonstrate the importance of good work habits. You can do this by making sure employees understand the consequences of their actions.

Sally's manager had received a vigorous complaint from a customer about poor quality. Instead of reprimanding Sally, who was responsible for the less-than-perfect work, or trying to defend his operation to the customer, the manager sent Sally to visit the customer. He had done this before on a selective basis and in almost every case the complaints had stopped.

In this instance, however, the results were even better. The formerly dissatisfied customer called to compliment Sally. "She apologized and corrected her work," the customer related, "but she did a lot more than that. After seeing how we used her component, she suggested how we might redesign our product and cut our costs. Fabulous!"

By handling the complaint in a creative way, the manager gave Sally the opportunity to make amends for her error by allowing her to take responsibility for her work. The customer was much more satisfied, elated even, than he would have been if the manager had simply tried to appease him. And Sally was motivated and challenged in her job rather than embarrassed and deflated as she would have been by a humiliating reprimand. The wise manager helped Sally turn failure into success.

You can also demonstrate the importance of good work habits by giving promotions and desirable work to those who are well-disciplined. The coach of a professional football team traded one of his stars for a player of seeming lesser ability. Outsiders thought the coach had been outsmarted at his bargaining. But insiders knew that the star was actually an undisciplined individual whose wealth of native ability could not offset the damage he did to team spirit.

Build teamwork and team spirit. When you establish rapport with your people, you are on the way to team play. Next you need objectives. Then you need rewards to show that achieving the goals is worthwhile. When you have these working for you, good discipline will be a natural result.

One company won an order to build parts for the spacecraft that took John Glenn on the first orbit of the earth. The employees got so enthusiastic about this order that they turned it out in record time. The rapport was there, the objectives were clear, and the thrill of participating, even in a minor way, in one of the major adventures of the twentieth century was the satisfying reward. The employees had superb discipline, although they may not have thought of it as that. Team spirit brings about the best kind of discipline—the kind that is self-administered.

Demonstrate self-discipline. Managers who lose their tempers, get drunk on the job, or otherwise behave badly will have trouble disciplining their employees.

But the common examples of lack of self-discipline involve smaller and subtler problems. Supervisors who can't resist "riding" some employees, who can't control their tempers, who get emotional in a crisis will be the ones who have an unusual number of disciplinary problems to contend with. This occurs for the same reason that undisciplined parents are likely to have undisciplined children.

Some managers cannot control their pessimism and criticism. They have deep concerns about the course of the business and the abilities of top management to weather economic storms. But they don't voice such alarms to their superiors—only to their employees. If the concern is solidly based, little remedy can come from below. The communication should be upward, not downward. When supervisors do this downward griping, they succeed only in upsetting people. Negative behavior then thrives.

Be consistent. The same basic rules of behavior should apply to all. Another variety of poor self-discipline among managers, favoritism, can cause much dissension. Managers will inevitably like some people more than others, but they cannot afford to show personal preferences. Some well-meaning managers overbalance on this score. They make the rules tougher for their favorites than for others, using the muddy reasoning that the favorite has advantages just because he or she is the favorite. Yet, the favorite may not even know it.

Besides having the same rules for all, make sure all the rules are logical. It makes little sense to forbid smoking on the job if you are lax about other fire or health hazards, or vice versa.

Make the rules of behavior clear. Yet have as few rules as possible and be sure they are important. Commonly observed rules of decent behavior need not be spelled out, but should be enforced vigorously and promptly on an individual basis if violated. Starting time, break times, and quitting time are examples of rules that should be posted because they vary.

A manager reprimanded a secretary who consistently arrived at 9:15 every morning. "But I'm only fifteen minutes late," she rebutted.

"You're thirty minutes late. Our starting time is 8:45."

"I thought it was 9; that's when most everybody else arrives."

The supervisor had to admit that the rule about starting at 8:45 was widely ignored and perhaps even unknown by some, so the reprimand lost much of its point.

The case seems obvious and even trivial, but some people overlook the obvious and trivial. State your rules orally from time to time. Post them in a conspicuous place. Then practice what you preach and insist that your people do likewise.

A well-managed work unit will also be well-disciplined, and will rarely need to be reprimanded. A poorly managed, poorly disciplined unit is one that the supervisor must frequently chastise.

> He who heeds discipline shows the way to life, but whoever ignores correction leads others astray.
> — Proverbs 10:17

Lord, when I must punish, let me do it fairly and effectively.

Ideally, a well-disciplined unit need never be punished. But we can only approach the ideal, rarely achieve it. Inevitably, the unpleasant task of punishment will come up. How to deal with it? The following pointers may help you do the job fairly and effectively:

1. **Make sure the punishment is deserved.** Has the offender been warned previously that continued bad behavior would lead to punishment? Have similar offenses by others been punished? Has the previous warning notice been put in writing and attached to the offender's personnel file? These questions are always important, but particularly so in a unionized environment because the lack of a tangible warning or precedence will work against you in grievance and arbitration procedures.

Is the offender truly trying to reform or is he or she defiant and cynical? Has the offender a long history of other offenses? Are there extenuating circumstances, such as poor health or misunderstanding, that you should consider? The answer to these questions will help you determine the nature of the punishment.

Is the punishment you plan consistent with company practice? Have you consulted with your superior to let him know your proposed action and why you believe you must do it? Does the proposed punishment fit the crime? Most employers have schedules of punishments, ranging from one day off without pay to dismissal. If no one but Solomon could decide whether or not the punishment was just, it is usually best to take the most lenient course.

2. **Punish only as the last resort.** Have you tried talking to the offender about the problem? Do you know the fundamental factors that cause the objectionable

behavior? Have you offered to help work out problems? If an employee misbehaves out of carelessness, laziness, or because he or she doesn't know any better, you may be able to relieve the problem without punishing—just by reasoning.

3. **Keep the punishment private.** There is rarely any need to publicize the event as an object lesson to others. Other employees will soon know the circumstances because negative news always leaks out. But be sure you don't do the leaking. The usual source of such information is the offender. Let him or her spread the word. Your punishment must be just because God demands it, but so do your other employees, and you can be sure they will judge its fairness as soon as they hear of it.

Knowing that the offender will talk about the case with others, you are wise to keep your ear to the ground to assure yourself that he or she tells an accurate story.

In addition to being just in your punishment, you should carefully keep your own sense of proportion in dealing out the chastisement. Hold your temper. Say nothing you will regret later. Avoid vindictiveness.

The only time you should make public a case of punishment is when it is dismissal. Then, when the offender has left, explain the circumstances and tell precisely why you had to act.

4. **Follow up to be sure the offense is not committed again.** The purpose of punishment is to help the offender reform. Punishment that does not achieve that result is useless. If you sincerely believe that more punishment will serve no further purpose, discharge the employee. But if he or she is salvageable, follow up—with compassion and humility. You could salvage an employee who will turn out to be a star performer.

According to the dictionary, punishment is "a penalty inflicted on an offender as a retribution and for reformation and prevention." Usually, such a penalty involves a tangible loss or forfeit, such as time off without pay.

With many people and in certain circumstances, you can get good or better results with a reprimand that involves no tangible penalty. Some people take a reprimand more to heart than a penalty because it hits their pride—a more vulnerable spot than their pocket.

Although Christ's words in Matthew 18 were spoken to believers in the setting of the church, they are applicable to managers in a business setting.

> If your brother sins against you, go and show him his fault, just between the two of you. If he listens to you, you have won your brother over. But if he will not listen, take one or two others along, so that "every matter may be established by the testimony of two or three witnesses." If he refuses to listen to them, tell it to the church; and if he refuses to listen even to the church, treat him as you would a pagan or a tax collector. — Matthew 18:15–17

Lord, give me the skill to criticize honestly and fairly.

Most of us don't like to criticize, but sometimes it is essential to stop an undesirable practice among employees. Some managers avoid ever placing blame. If they supervise so well and have such good people that no mistakes ever get made, more power to them. But most of us are not so talented. Occasionally, the necessity to censure is forced upon us. Here are suggestions on how to do the job right:

1. **Keep it impersonal, private, and fair.** Talk about the job, not the person.

2. **Listen.** Evaluate and accept as much as possible of the employee's explanation for the error.

3. **Plan the perfect timing for your censure.** Do not delay, but don't be hasty either. Do it as soon after the error or the objectionable practice as possible, but not before you have given sufficient thought to the form of your criticism.

4. **Do not delegate to others the task of reprimanding.** The person reproved will interpret delegation as cowardice on your part or evidence that the error is not serious.

5. **Do not be apologetic about the reproof.** The misdoer will react the same as if you had delegated the job.

6. **Be positive in your reprimand.** Say why the error is serious or the practice unacceptable. Show how to solve the problem. Offer your help.

7. **Avoid ultimatums except in extreme cases.** They put both you and the employee in a corner which may lead to no course but discharge for the employee. The ultimatum is rarely needed because anyone of average intelligence and common sense will know what failure to reform can mean. Distinguish carefully between willful, careless, and ignorant mistakes.

8. **Assure the offender of your continuing personal respect, if you can honestly do so.** This should come near the end of the reprimand and should underscore the fact that you differentiate between the error and the individual.

9. **Follow up.** Check that the same error or malpractice does not occur again. If it does, take more forceful action. Make your reprimand stick.

10. **Watch out for the addictive effect criticizing others may have on you.** Just as some people can't take too

much alcohol without its having a harmful effect on their personalities, others can't deal out censure without becoming addicted to the practice. If you see this as a possible problem for you, dole out your reprimands sparingly. Even so, remain always on guard.

> He who heeds discipline shows the way to life, but whoever ignores correction leads others astray.
> — Proverbs 10:17

DOUBTS

Lord, don't spare me from doubts (or doubters) because they give me my real education.

After Christ's crucifixion and resurrection, he came to some of his disciples and showed them his hands and side. Thomas, a cautious, skeptical man, was not among them.

> When the other disciples told him [Thomas] that they had seen the Lord, he declared, "Unless I see the nail marks in his hands and put my finger where the nails were, and put my hand into his side, I will not believe it."
> A week later his disciples were in the house again, and Thomas was with them. Though the doors were locked, Jesus came and stood among them and said, "Peace be with you!" Then he said to Thomas, "Put your finger here; see my hands. Reach out your hand and put it into my side. Stop doubting and believe."
> Thomas said to him, "My Lord and my God!" Then Jesus told him, "Because you have seen me, you have believed; blessed are those who have not seen and yet have believed."
> — John 20:25–29

Doubting is a valuable characteristic. We need skeptics. Without them, we would have fewer believers. Skeptics demand proof. They force us to be more sure of ourselves and of our tightly held beliefs and opinions. It is often from doubters that we get our education in faith.

EMPATHY

Lord, grant me empathy for others.

Empathy is defined as "the mental identification of the ego with the character and experiences of another person." It is probably more enduring and valuable than romantic love. All divorces have at their root a lack of empathy between the partners.

Yet the magic of empathy lies in the fact that it need not involve love in the romantic sense, just understanding.

A supervisor recommended that a competent young woman working in the backroom of a bank be promoted to a position as teller where her pleasant personality and appearance might better serve herself and the institution. In her new job, she became subject to severe sneezing spells. The doctor found that the woman was allergic to money. She had to return to check processing until a position in personal loan applications could be found for her.

"I knew I had the problem," she later confessed, "but the supervisor was so pleased with himself to get me promoted to teller that I hated to disappoint him." The supervisor had little empathy with the young woman, and neither did she with him.

Empathy doesn't just happen. It must be developed. The best ways to nurture it are to be honest and to listen.

Honesty does not mean brutal frankness. It means revealing part of yourself to another by showing some of your own emotions and attitudes. This is not easy because most of us have been taught throughout our lives to hide our true feelings. We do this because we have learned that a close friend can be as much of a burden as a bitter enemy. But we must accept the burdens of friendship if we want empathic communication.

Empathic listening becomes part of this as well. If the supervisor had been really listening to the young woman, he may have heard a whisper or a hint about her problem. And she should have been more forthright and honest in revealing her problem to him.

> *A generous man will prosper; he who refreshes others will himself be refreshed.* — Proverbs 11:25

FEAR

Lord, if I am cowardly, chastise me; but if I am fearful, support me.

A French colonel punished a young officer one day for showing fear during his first battle. Marshal Foch, to whose notice it came, severely reprimanded the disciplinarian. "Colonel!" he said, "none but a coward dares to boast that he has never known fear!"

The most common form of cowardice a manager shows is trying to hide mistakes for fear of reprisal. Errors seldom escape eventual detection. Admit them, correct them, try not to make the same mistake again.

As to cowardice in others: the coward dies a thousand deaths; the hero just one. So the coward inflicts the worst punishment on himself.

Perhaps Abraham Lincoln's attitude is best. He was often the despair of his generals for his lenient treatment of soldiers absent without leave. "If the good Lord has given a man a cowardly pair of legs," the President reasoned, "it is hard to keep them from running away with him."

Fear as we usually think of it is a distressing emotion that is brought on by impending pain, danger, or evil, either real or imagined. Because fear is unpleasant and counter-productive, we do our best to avoid it, as we should in most cases. But Scripture speaks of a legitimate fear—a fear we should not try to relieve, a fear that is indeed necessary for wisdom: the fear of God. Without it, all our other fears will never be allayed.

> The fear of the Lord is the beginning of knowledge, but fools despise wisdom and discipline. . . . But whoever listens to me will live in safety and be at ease, without fear of harm.
> — Proverbs 1:7, 33

Lord, teach me to overcome fear, especially job-related.

> The Lord is my shepherd; I shall lack nothing.
>   He makes me lie down in green pastures,
> he leads me beside quiet waters,

> he restores my soul.
> He guides me in paths of righteousness
> > for his name's sake.
> Even though I walk
> > through the valley of the shadow of death,
> I will fear no evil,
> > for you are with me;
> your rod and your staff,
> > they comfort me.
>
> You prepare a table before me
> > in the presence of my enemies.
> You anoint my head with oil;
> > my cup overflows.
> Surely goodness and love will follow me
> > all the days of my life,
> and I will dwell in the house of the Lord
> > forever.
>
> — Psalm 23

Lord, when my fear reaches an unhealthy level, help me to admit it to you and to others who may be able to help me overcome it.

Ted performed well as a salesman for business forms and supplies, but fears often dogged him. He often felt he should try the administrative side of marketing, but he had never asked for such a move. With good reason, he believed his employer valued him too highly on the line to give him a chance to achieve that ambition. At other times, he felt he lacked talent for anything but "peddling." Once or twice a year, usually when he lost a good sale, he fought fits of depression. When his firm hired new salesmen, he viewed them as rivals, despite the fact that he was the perennial top salesman for the company and had had no serious rivals in years.

Is Ted some kind of nut? Perhaps. But if he is, a lot of others are too. One in eight Americans will suffer a bout of depression serious enough to need psychiatric help during his or her lifetime. According to the National Institute of Mental Health, 125,000 Americans are hospitalized each year with depression, while another 200,000 are treated on psychiatrists' couches or in physicians' offices. No figures exist for the number who seek help from clergy. Perhaps they are included in the estimated four to eight million who need assistance but don't go to medical doctors. Ted fell within this group.

Depression has been diagnosed by physicians at least since Hippocrates. The disorder has afflicted many notable figures in history—Winston Churchill, Abraham Lincoln, Vincent van Gogh, and numerous others. But studies of those who patronize free psychiatric clinics indicate that depression knows no boundaries set by talent or economics. It hits anyone.

Depression's irony lies in the fact that it drives some people to prodigious effort and achievement. When Ted suffered periodic bouts of depression, he usually chalked up his best sales performances. Yet his depression also left him tired and apathetic about his family and other non-job responsibilities.

Although there is no magic formula to relieve depression, psychotherapeutic techniques, drugs, and electroshock therapy have brought dramatic relief to many. Ted tried none of these. He went to his minister. Among the practical advice the minister gave was that Ted ask his employer for a trial in marketing administration. "They can say no, at the worst," he advised. "If they do, you can decide if you want to leave them for someone who will give you a trial. But you need to answer the question: Can I make it as a manager? If you learn you can, fine. If you learn you cannot, you know you can still be an excellent salesman. You first have to learn what you are. When you do, then you can accept limitations, if any."

In addition to fears of failure, Ted also feared that he wouldn't be able to make as much money at a new job. So his minister also reminded him of some Scriptural concepts concerning finances and of God's promise to care for his children who trust him.

> Keep your lives free from the love of money and be content with what you have, because God has said, "Never will I leave you; never will I forsake you." So we say with confidence, "The Lord is my helper; I will not be afraid. What can man do to me?" — Hebrews 13:5–6

FEEDBACK

Lord, let me know what my employees are saying, thinking, doing, and planning, for am I not their leader?

By developing good feedback from your employees you can learn how you are scoring. The best gauge of your performance is the overall job your employees do. If they don't do well, look to your ability to communicate for at least part of the reason. Even if they do well, check regularly on how you're getting across. You can always do better.

Besides poor job performance, many other indications hint at feedback gone awry. These include high absenteeism, a poor safety record, substantial turnover, scarce suggestions, many grievances, numerous work stoppages and disciplinary problems, and low participation in voluntary benefit plans.

Beware, however, because many of these signals come after the fact. You need faster signs of trouble, or success. One approach: Win such high confidence and respect from your employees that they will tell you promptly if you are not coming through. But they won't feed back to you automatically. Let them know you want their reactions, even when unfavorable.

Often one employee will be particularly perceptive in noting reactions, so he or she can serve as your sounding board. You too can observe how your arguments fare. Put all these indications together, and you can have an efficient feedback system.

Continuing feedback is a necessity because people and situations change. George Bernard Shaw expressed this problem when he wrote: "The only man who behaves sensibly is my tailor; he takes my dimensions anew every time he sees me whilst all the rest go on with the old measurements, and expect them to fit me."

Measure your employees periodically. Even last week's results may be out of date now.

Don't talk so much yourself that you allow no opportunity for feedback. Your position as a manager may contribute to excessive talking because employees naturally will defer to you. If you have a tendency to be a chatterbox, you may be encouraged in your foibles because people will conceal from you some of the usual signs of boredom.

> Be sure you know the condition of your flocks, give careful attention to your herds; for riches do not endure forever, and a crown is not secure for all generations.
> — Proverbs 27:23–24

Lord, may my feedback system help me reward the competent, reform the careless, and deal objectively with the incompetent.

Feedback is part of, but different from, an appraisal system, either formal or informal. Feedback is the information you gather to use in making judgments. The more informal the feedback, the better. And the ideal feedback occurs when employees, as a matter of course, question what you say when they don't agree or don't understand.

Besides the free flow of information from your employees—by far your most important suppliers—many other sources are available. Among them:

- Suggestion plans, Speak Up programs, and other similar methods of soliciting employee ideas, complaints, and comments.

- Absenteeism trends—declines indicate good things are happening; increases the opposite.

- Trends in rework and customer complaints—down is good; up is bad.

- Suggestion and other incentive awards—down is bad; up is good.

- Unit and overall profit trends—down is bad; up is good.

Managers *supply* feedback as well as receive it from their employees. Handing out incentive awards, giving orders, complimenting good performances, and reinforcing employees who need to modify their directions are forms of managerial feedback. This type of feedback, usually quick and casual, can clarify employee rules in the organization and serve as a mini-appraisal. Be restrained, however, in using it for this function.

Also, remember that when you give feedback it is effective chiefly when you are specific, friendly and constructive, when you have credibility, and when you occupy a position of stature.

> Preserve sound judgment and discernment, do not let them out of your sight; they will be life for you, an ornament to grace your neck. Then you will go on your way in safety, and your foot will not stumble; when you lie down, you will not be afraid; when you lie down, your sleep will be sweet.
> — Proverbs 3:21–24

Lord, help me with upward feedback, not just downward.

One of the challenges managers face is how to communicate effectively with their bosses, as well as with the people working for them. In fact, upward and downward feedback go together like computer software and hardware. Without the rapport and support of the boss, managers can achieve little with their own people.

When you accept the importance of balanced upward

feedback, the next question to arise is: Communicate what? What you need to communicate is what your boss wants and needs to know. Your challenge is to figure out most of what that is without explicit directions. This involves knowing almost as much about the job as the boss does. Usually, you should keep your superior carefully informed on matters like this:

1. **Areas for which your superior is accountable.** If you see you can't get an assignment done on time, if you know you will exceed your budget, if you can't perform the work in the way originally contemplated, let the boss know at once because he or she is accountable upward in such matters. Similarly, inform your boss if you *can* meet deadlines, budgets, and original plans.

2. **Matters that need top management's approval and/or knowledge.** If you see a way to do an assignment differently and less expensively than planned, let your superior know. And look before you leap in areas involving policy and practice. This also applies to matters about which your boss would want to alert top brass—developments such as strikes, workforce expansions or contractions, government actions affecting your organization, etc.

3. **Projects you are pursuing.** Give work highlights, progress, and future plans. Do the same for your subordinates. Do it often enough to keep your superior current, but not so often that you are repetitious or boring. Always report promptly any change in the status of your projects.

4. **Unresolved or new problems.** The new problems, particularly, often mean bad news. Naturally, many people postpone talking to the boss about them. Don't delay a minute. Your superior may have the answer at

hand (or may be able to find it more readily than you) to solve a problem before it becomes major.

5. **Suggestions for improvements.** This is the responsibility of every manager. The boss who cuts these off doesn't belong on the job. But don't expect to bat a thousand in getting your suggestions approved. An average of three hundred is phenomenal; one hundred is more like it in this league.

6. **How you and your subordinates think and feel about your jobs.** Unfortunately, most of us give little attention to this in upward feedback. It is meaningless to communicate platitudes upward: "I'm very happy . . . a very rewarding job . . . everything's going fine." Talk frankly and objectively about your job with your boss. Encourage your own people to do likewise with you so that you can pass this on too.

7. **Legitimate grievances of your people.** This relates to the sixth point, but it goes in a somewhat different direction than simply discussing job attitudes. These are specific grievances, usually with high emotional content. Your people want redress. To keep your credibility with them, you must satisfy them. If you can't solve it yourself, take it to your superior. This is an acid test of upward feedback because your boss may resent having to deal with such problems. So, it is important that you first try to resolve the difficulties. If you fail, come to your superior armed with suggestions of what to do.

Managers are not mindreaders; we cannot expect them to understand or solve our problems unless we communicate with them. Even God, who *can* read our minds and who knows every thought we think, wants us to communicate with him.

> "Call upon me in the day of trouble; I will deliver you, and you will honor me." — Psalm 50:15

FINANCIAL ANALYSIS

Lord, grant me to the *nth* degree the power of analysis, especially financial analysis.

Business management's success is measured in terms of profit. In turn, profit is measured in a variety of ways, each of which recognizes the need to relate the profit dollars earned to some supporting structure assumed to have provided the means of earning the profit itself.

The various ways to measure profitability include:

- **The ratio of earnings to sales.** This is usually expressed as a percentage of the net book earnings after taxes measured against the net dollar volume of sales recorded for the same fiscal period. The resulting percent-to-sales ratio is often compared to prior periods as well as to forecasts and budgets; it provides a useful measure of trends.

- **Dollars and cents earned per share of common stock.** This is arrived at by taking the net book earnings after taxes and dividing by the average number of shares of common stock outstanding during the period. This, too, is compared with similar earnings in prior periods and is essentially an evaluation from the investor's, rather than management's, viewpoint.

- **Net book earnings after taxes as a percentage of the total equity investment or net worth of the company.** This method usually plays a secondary role in financial analysis because it normally presents a more moderate picture of annual growth in earnings than does the first approach.

- **Rate of return on invested capital.** Management generally considers this the best measure because it recognizes that (a) all capital has a cost; (b) the total cost of total capital used—regardless of source—is commensurate with the composite risk at which the capital is used; and (c) a company to be truly profitable must recover all costs, including the cost of capital.

Return on invested capital, at least in larger companies, can also be applied to individual profit centers within the corporate structure—another attribute of the fourth method that makes it attractive to management. This is accomplished by translating the corporate objective for a net after-tax rate of return on total invested capital into the contributing pretax rate of return required from a particular segment of the business. The operating results at the profit center are typically measured in terms of profit contribution.

It is important for every manager to learn at least the basics of accounting language. Without this basic knowledge it is impossible to communicate in the business community, and a lack of communication will inevitably lead to failure.

The Bible teaches us a lesson about the importance of communication. Remember the story of the Tower of Babel. The people of Shinar decided to build themselves "a tower that reaches to the heavens, so that we may make a name for ourselves. . . . " God knew they could accomplish this evil goal if they could communicate with one another, so he confused their languages.

> The Lord said, "If as one people speaking the same language they have begun to do this, then nothing they plan to do will be impossible for them. Come, let us go down and confuse their language so they will not understand each other."
> — Genesis 11:6–7

Lord, remind me that accountants never die, they just count away.

Non-financial people should never forget this truth: Accounting procedures are growing increasingly important and essential in both the public and private sectors. Here is a common example:

FIFO (first in, first out) and LIFO (last in, first out) are two forms of inventory accounting. Under FIFO, you assign costs to units sold in the same order as the costs entered the inventory. As a result, during periods of rising prices, the older and therefore lower costs are subtracted from revenue when you determine your reported and therefore taxable earnings.

Under LIFO, you remove your newest costs from the top and assign them to units sold. Unless the bottom layer of costs is liquidated by sale of inventories, it can remain on the books indefinitely. So, during periods of rising prices, the older and therefore lower costs remain in the balance-sheet inventory while you use the newer and higher costs to calculate earnings.

Compared to FIFO, reported earnings under LIFO

FINANCIAL ANALYSIS

will usually drop—but so do taxes on earnings. Although a company will have more cash available for operations or dividend distribution, its published profits will be lower.

Who but an accountant should care about this? Everyone, because it affects our financial well-being.

FORGIVENESS

Lord, when an employee quits, shall I take him back?

A certain man had two employees. The one with shorter service said to him as soon as he was vested, "Boss, give me the portion of the savings plan that falls to me, and I will take my pension as soon as I'm sixty."

The employee with shorter service found another employer in a far city, and there wasted his substance.

When he had spent all from the savings plan, his new employer suffered declining business and laid him off. He went on unemployment compensation, but that soon ran out.

Then he said, "My former boss prospers. I'll return to him."

He said to his former boss, "I have erred. I should never have left you. If you take me back, make me your lowest paid employee."

But the boss said, "I welcome you and need your skills. I feared I had lost you forever."

Now the employee with longer service was angry and said to the boss, "I have served you many years, never transgressing. Yet, you have never honored me as you do him."

And the boss said to him, "My friend, you are ever with me, your savings plan is building up, your pension is rising, and your pay scale is increasing steadily, much more than for the other. It was proper that we should welcome him, for he was dead and is alive again, and was lost and is found."

— Adapted from Luke 15:11–32

GOALS/OBJECTIVES

Lord, never allow me to base my career on the gratitude of others.

Each of us needs to achieve the right balance between the way others want us to perform and the way we are actually motivated. Our motivation to achieve goes along with our professional approach to job performance. Our jobs are both a paid service to our company and a vehicle for our advancement. In the coming months do the following to evaluate your strengths and weaknesses:

- Define your real interests in life. Do this by analyzing your present work and all your former jobs; list the things you like and dislike about specific job activities.

- Assess your special skills and abilities. Do this by reviewing all your educational experiences; list areas in which you consistently received high marks and recall commendations from teachers. This exercise is to identify aptitudes, not to give you an ego trip!

- Analyze your work history and look for those things you are particularly proud of and the skills you brought to those projects.

Once you have defined and recorded your interests and talents, you will have a better idea of who you really are, not just who others think you are.

> The Lord does not look at the things man looks at. Man looks at the outward appearance, but the Lord looks at the heart. — 1 Samuel 16:7

> Now it is required that those who have been given a trust must prove faithful. I care very little if I am judged by you or by any human court.... It is the Lord who judges me.... He will bring to light what is hidden in darkness and will expose the motives of men's hearts. — 1 Corinthians 4:2–5

Lord, never let success go to my head, nor failure to my heart.

Sometimes we forget that every experience, failure as well as success, comes through God.

> In his heart a man plans his course, but the Lord determines his steps. — Proverbs 16:9

Lord, never let me become fully satisfied because then I'll be a failure.

Even the most stimulating job can become boring if we allow ourselves to function strictly from habit and never challenge ourselves to come up with new ideas or ways of doing things. Without a conscious effort to keep our jobs interesting we will go toward one of two extremes: carelessness or perfectionism. If we allow everyday tasks to become routine, we are likely to become careless in the way we handle them; on the other hand, however, we may try to keep routine jobs from becoming boring by becoming too perfectionistic in the way we handle them. Neither extreme is good.

Here are some suggestions to help us maintain a sense of moderation:

- List all activities that are no longer challenging. For each activity, make at least three suggestions to add new life to the task. Choose the most practical and follow through.

- Divide the more complex suggestions into component parts and tackle them one at a time.

- Make every effort to keep *all* goals and deadlines in mind to keep from getting bogged down in unnecessary detail.

Above all, remember that success has made failures of many men.

Lord, keep me from both over-reaching and under-achieving.

Most business experts agree that goals, to be effective, should be specific and preferably quantitative. For example, reduce costs by seven percent.

There is less agreement, however, on the issue of the ideal level of goal difficulty. One view holds that moderately difficult goals will produce the highest performance because low goals will produce low performance and high goals allegedly will produce discouragement and apathy as a result of repeated failures.

Actually, numerous research studies have found that difficult, specific goals lead to better performance than either moderate or easy goals.

However, it is possible to over-reach. This usually results from setting poor objectives or from having none at all, except for a burning but unfocused desire to "get ahead."

Typically, the over-reacher has many outstanding abilities, makes good initial impressions, and is highly ambitious. Yet often he or she is ruthless with others, has poor judgment and takes foolish risks, has trouble working with others, and has no notion that over-ambition even is possible.

> A faithful man will be richly blessed, but one eager to get rich will not go unpunished. — Proverbs 28:20

> If you find honey, eat just enough—too much of it, and you will vomit. — Proverbs 25:16

Lord, grant me persistence, insistence, and assistance in achieving goals that are right for me and the people dependent on me.

Objectives are defined as general statements of what the organization must do to accomplish its purpose, including the limits—markets, product lines, geographic areas and distribution channels—within which it will operate. Goals are the specific things that must be accomplished to achieve business objectives.

The process of developing goals and objectives differs from organization to organization, depending on the structure and degree of decentralization of the organization. The process is repetitious because it must incorporate feedback from each stage in the planning procedure.

As a manager, therefore, you need persistence, insistence, and assistance as in no other organizational operation:

- Persistence just to get the job done.

- Insistence to assure that you win reasonable and equitable goals and objectives for your own department.

- Assistance from your own employees to develop a doable plan and from your peers to get the resources necessary to accomplish the goals and objectives.

> For lack of guidance a nation falls, but many advisers make victory sure. — Proverbs 11:14

Lord, let me concentrate on the important; the trivial will usually look after itself.

"The true, strong and sound mind is the mind that can embrace equally great things and small," said Samuel Johnson more than two centuries ago. Note that he said small, not trivial. Small things can be as important as great things. (And great things may be trivial.)

Today trivia is put on a pedestal as something great. *Trivial Pursuit* is a best-selling game. Professors intone that "trivia is American folklore." Books on trivia abound. Trivia may be amusing, interesting, and entertaining, but it is not important. So usually let it look after itself.

Lord, let me not discover that my goals and objectives are trivial. If I do, help me transform them into something important.

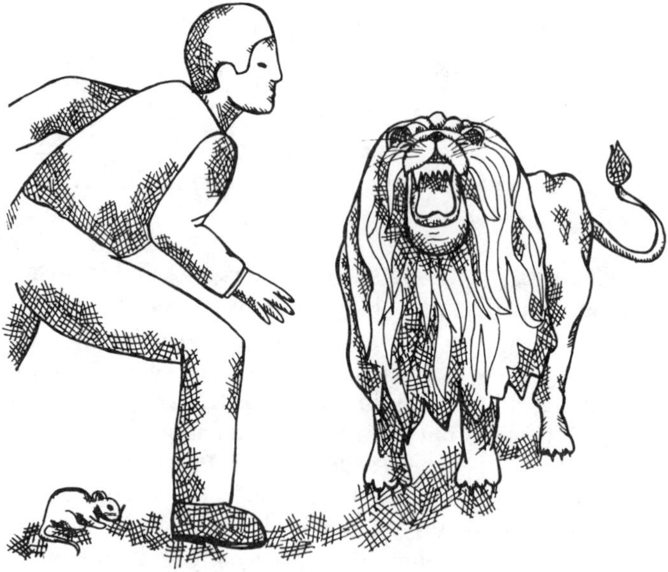

> "Woe to you, teachers of the law and Pharisees, you hypocrites! You give a tenth of your spices—mint, dill and cummin. But you have neglected the more important matters of the law—justice, mercy and faithfulness."
> — Matthew 23:23

Lord, help me know where I'm going, so I don't end up where I don't belong.

"Our plans miscarry because they have no aim. When a man does not know what harbor he is making for, no wind is the right wind," said Seneca twenty-one centuries ago.

"We must ask where we are and where we are tending," said Abraham Lincoln twelve decades ago.

A large corporation set a new-product marketing objective that would involve high research-and-development costs for two years and high marketing costs the third year to introduce the product. Management set a financial goal of an average annual return on investment of fourteen percent over six years.

Financial analysts evaluated the new-product investment and recommended that the project be abandoned because the business objective and the financial goal were inconsistent. However, the engineering vice president whose department had developed the product persuaded the president to overrule the financial analysts on the grounds that they had overestimated initial development expenses.

Alas! The financial analysis was right. The project proved to be an expensive fiasco.

As Thomas Carlyle said a century ago, "Nothing is more terrible than activity without insight."

GREED

Lord, keep me from greed.

Wes groped for the ringing telephone beside his bed and greeted the caller with a sleepy hello.

"Harshman of the *News,*" came the voice on the line. "Sorry to wake you up at this hour, but we've just got wind of a development in welfare that we need your comment on."

Wes grimaced as he squinted at his bedside clock radio. Six-thirty—an hour before he normally got up. "No trouble, Jim. What's the problem?" He had met Harshman only once but had spoken to him on the phone a few times. Harshman was the author of many by-lined articles for the city's largest newspaper, including a recent series uncomplimentary to the commissioner, Wes's boss. Publicly Wes had deplored them, but privately he welcomed them because they might help his own ambitions.

"We understand," the reporter said, "that the Welfare Department is going to start a new system of validating welfare clients in order to cut relief rolls by ten percent."

"Jim, my hat's off to you. You have *some* sources!"

"What's the score?"

"Jim, you put me on the spot. I can't comment yet, as you must know." Wes was in more of a spot than Harshman could have realized. Wes knew nothing about any fresh validation program. Proposals of this sort floated around the department most of the time. Anything could happen, but he had not been privy to

GREED

anything new, to his distress. Although validation proposals didn't originate in his shop, any reporter would expect him to have inside information as the assistant commissioner in charge of public relations. Wes felt gratified that Harshman had called him, especially because the reporter had ignored him and his press releases for months. His predecessor in the job had won good coverage from the *News*. Wes wished to exploit this opening.

"Does the rumor stand?" Harshman asked brusquely.

"We've considered several validation methods recently."

Harshman openly voiced his disgust. Wes thought hard. The veteran reporter could help him in his climb to the top in the welfare agency. The paper could prove valuable in supporting him, Wes, for the job if he recruited allies like Harshman from its staff. He had already received favorable notice in the interviews by reporters from the city's other paper and TV stations.

At twenty-eight, he was by far the youngest assistant commissioner in any of the city's score of agencies. His meteoric rise in only four years as a civil servant resulted from a combination of luck, ability, and another quality that the mayor referred to when he said, "Wes has more brass than a burglar."

That characteristic had caught His Honor's attention three and a half years earlier. The mayor was up for his fourth consecutive four-year term and astutely recognized that he had to project an image of youth and freshness through others, not himself. So, he scoured his bureaucracy and found Wes languishing in the Health Department with a new Master's degree in public administration. Wes helped him in his campaign. The mayor won, and so did Wes—the assistant commissionership in Welfare, supplanting Jones in public relations. Yet, things had not gone well since then. He had trouble with the administrative aspects of his position, and he found himself in several embarrassing mix-ups. The mayor had cooled toward him and not invited him to help in his fifth re-election campaign. Wes needed to recoup.

"Well, what about it?" rasped Harshman.

Wes realized with a start that he had remained silent for nearly a minute as he thought of ways to regain His Honor's sponsorship, perhaps with the help of the reporter and his paper. "Sorry, Jim. I was mulling over the best way I could help you. Can you hold off on this for twenty-four hours?" Harshman objected to the delay. "But it will be exclusive to you, Jim." Wes wheedled and pleaded, yet the reporter adamantly held out for confirmation or denial. Afraid both of appearing stupid and of alienating Harshman, Wes said, "Okay, you can confirm it but don't quote me now. Later, yes, in twenty-four hours." Harshman agreed to that and at last hung up.

At home that evening, Harshman called again. "I've got to have more. Did you see the *Post?* They're getting antsy, too." Wes talked in circles, but ended thinking he had placated Harshman without saying anything. He was wrong. The next morning Wes had summonses from both the commissioner's and the mayor's offices. He answered the mayor's first. His Honor had the *News* before him with the Harshman story. "Wes, you look ridiculous in this story. And you make the administration look ridiculous. Every welfare protective group in the city has called me wanting to know what this means. Did Harshman quote you right?"

"He quoted me completely out of context."

The mayor looked at Wes quizzically. "Harshman played the tapes over to me. I think he quoted you right. You sounded like an idiot. By extension, so do I." The mayor rose. The interview was over. "And Wes, you need a vacation. Take your two weeks starting right now. When you're back, come in and see me. We'll have something to talk over."

That evening in a small restaurant frequented by *News* staff, Jones, the former Welfare Department assistant commissioner for public relations, and Harshman enjoyed a steak dinner together.

"My sources tell me that friend Wes got canned today," said the reporter through a mouthful of beef.

"You gonna print that?" Jones asked eagerly.

"I dunno. You gave me some real stuff on the commissioner, but this was more like a trick on the miserable kid."

Jones leaned forward, his face flushed. "Miserable kid, nothing. Greedy kid. Didn't I tell you he'd snap at the bait? Come on. Let's finish him off."

Harshman looked thoughtfully at the other. "Cousin, Jonesy, I did this as a favor to my mother's sister's boy. But enough's enough." He paused. "There are all kinds of greed, ya know. Another kind is revenge."

> A greedy man stirs up dissension, but he who trusts in the Lord will prosper. — Proverbs 28:25

HEALTH SERVICES

Lord, let me devote as much effort to maintaining health as to curing sickness.

Employee injuries and illnesses adversely affect compensation, absenteeism, and turnover costs. And they leave employers wide open for inspections and possible citations under the Occupational Safety and Health Act of 1970.

What can we do to maintain health and minimize employee injuries? There are no magic answers or formulas, just commonsense approaches such as these:

- Offer stop-smoking, stress-reduction, and weight-reduction clinics to employees.

- Encourage employees to have regular medical examinations.

- Treat minor ailments and injuries on the premises.

- Conduct health-maintenance campaigns modeled after the highly successful safety programs that have made American work places among the safest in the world.

- Don't neglect health and safety maintenance programs. Everyone talks about the subject, but few do anything about it.

Reckless words pierce like a sword, but the tongue of the wise brings healing. — Proverbs 12:18

HIRING

Lord, help me keep good people after I hire them.

The truly effective employment program concentrates on seeking and hiring the best qualified candidates and on assimilating them into the organization as smoothly as possible.

The first step in assimilation is orientation. Depending on the size and complexity of the organization, an orientation program can be formal, including speakers and audiovisual presentations, or as informal as a one-on-one discussion.

The format isn't crucial, but the quantity and quality of information is. Surprisingly, you can err by giving too much information too quickly. If you have a complex benefit plan, explain it a little at a time over a period of weeks, confining the first session to insurance and related matters about which the new employee should decide quickly. It is not unreasonable to spread orientation meetings over two or three months. This gives new employees time to get their bearings and ask more relevant questions.

In quality, aim high and broadly. Give a brief history of the organization, stressing its emphasis on top performance. Detail wage and salary administration policies, benefits, work conditions, rules and regulations, and employee services.

And don't forget the new employee after orientation. Monitor progress, or assign someone else the task if you don't have time. The first year is especially crucial because the new employee will quit within that time if dissatisfied. The monitor should spot any signs of discontent and attempt to resolve them.

> Do you see a man skilled in his work? He will serve before kings; he will not serve before obscure men.
> — Proverbs 22:29

Lord, give me wisdom in hiring employees so that I am never caught in a position of having to fire any.

It has been said that the closest to perfection anyone comes is in filling out a job application form. The closest to perfection that managers come is in their ability to design a job application form and accurately evaluate it when it's filled out.

Except for interviews, application forms are the most widely used device for evaluating potential employees. Too frequently they are carelessly designed, many items in them "borrowed" from others. Items on the application blank should be determined by job analysis. Because of differences in job requirements, an employer may need several application forms for different types of jobs.

Four types of items are needed on application forms: (1) information required by law or needed for government reports and employee benefit programs; (2) information needed to communicate with the employee or his family; (3) personal information needed to match job requirements determined through job analysis and research; and (4) information to check the validity of the applicant's statements, such as names and addresses of organizations with whom the person has been previously employed, and names of former managers.

For positions that require a high level of education and cultural experiences, the application form should be tailor-made in wording and even appearance to take into account this fact.

Application forms should be attractive because they give candidates their first impression of an organization. In addition, they should be designed to permit maximum efficiency in handling, filing, and retrieving. Information on the forms should be organized so the forms are easy to use with an application checklist when a checklist is part of the screening procedure.

Evaluating applications requires managers to pay special attention to details. They must verify the information, a painstaking chore, and judge the veracity of the answers. Wise managers inform applicants that data supplied will be checked with original sources; usually that will discourage applicants from reporting false information. One government study revealed that errors or falsifications turned up on forty-six percent of the forms filled in by Civil Service applicants. In another study, reports of previous compensation were incorrect about half the time. Reasons listed for leaving previous jobs were also dubious in a significant number of cases.

> Like an archer who wounds at random is he who hires a fool or any passer-by. — Proverbs 26:10

Lord, when I am interviewing, teach me to see into the applicant's heart as well as mind.

A manager was biased against male secretaries. He thought something was wrong with the manhood of a male who took such a job. If he had been born a half-century earlier, he probably would have been the last to allow women in the office.

But he had an opening for a secretary. When he discovered one of the candidates was a man, he refused to see him until the personnel manager reminded him that laws concerning fair employment applied to males as well as females.

The manager found himself listening to the applicant. They both came from Enola, Pennsylvania, although three decades separated them in age. They agreed that the town's name should be changed (alone spelled backwards). They shared model railroading as a hobby (Enola being an early railroad center). The candidate was attending the University of Pittsburgh evenings, majoring in accounting, also the manager's field.

The manager surprised himself by hiring him on the spot. He never regretted his decision and later promoted him to his first job as an accountant in his own department.

IMAGINATION

Lord, give me plenty of dreams, because those who dream most do most.

One afternoon in 1865, Friedrich August von Kekule, professor of chemistry in Ghent, Belgium, sat dozing in his chair by the fire, dreaming of twisting atoms that became entwined in snakelike fashion. This fantasy led to the revolutionary suggestion that the molecules of certain important organic compounds were not open structures but were closed chains or "rings"—resembling the form of a snake swallowing its tail. Von Kekule's dream led to the clue to a discovery called "the most brilliant piece of prediction . . . in organic chemistry."

Much evidence exists that the subconscious plays a vital role in helping us make the creative leap. We can make three major deductions about how innovative people use their subconscious:

1. They deliberately give it full play.
2. They use it in a wordless way, by and large.
3. They use it to help them forget the obvious, the conventional.

Scientists who have studied dreaming report that the dreamer constantly jumps from one frame of reference to another, in leaps normally regarded as incompatible in the waking state. Dreamers drift effortlessly from matrix to matrix with no awareness. The fertile region appears to be the borderland between sleep and full awakening—a sort of "marshy shore"—where disciplined thought already operates but not yet with sufficient firmness to hamper the dream-like fluidity of imagination.

Many people seem to fear dreaming, abhorring it as a waste of time at the least, as immoral at the worst. They deliberately avoid daydreaming, even though they cannot prevent themselves from dreaming while asleep. This is not so for most creative individuals. They welcome the marshy shore because they know from experience that there they find gems of ideas. Unfortunately, many managers frown on reverie among their employees, not to mention themselves.

Despite the common prejudices against the marshy shore, you can develop deliberate ways to give the subconscious full play. Usually you need to bring it into play for only brief periods. As his research associates stood by, Charles P. Steinmetz, the German-born electrical engineering wizard, scribbled drawings that posed solutions to problems related to alternating current. But we ordinary people need to prepare to give our subconscious full play. Here are some suggestions:

Select an unhurried atmosphere. To summon the subconscious, you and your employees need a leisurely frame of mind. Find an atmosphere that suits you. The subconscious usually proves exasperatingly elusive. Interruptions and distractions force you to drop your train of thought when only your conscious mind is at work, but the subconscious mind is even more skittish. A celebrated case involves Otto Loewi, who discovered the chemical transmission of nerve impulses in animals. His subconscious mind had the first glimmer of the idea in 1903 in a reverie, but he forgot it, and his conscious mind took seventeen years to work it out. Allow innovative people to have periods without interruptions. Instruct them to use these times to start thinking about a problem. Jot down all ideas, even the most bizarre. Don't try to evaluate them. Keep pondering until frustration builds up. This often culminates in a flash of inspiration that leads to a workable solution.

Set a goal. When your conscious mind has an objective, your subconscious goes to work on it. To prove this, take paper and pencil and draw a circle around an average-size tumbler. Tie your house key to the end of a piece of string about six inches long. Hold the string and keep the key above the circle and think around the circle clockwise, ignoring the string and key. In a moment, the key will start swinging circularly clockwise. It will do the same if you think counterclockwise.

Prime the pump. Your subconscious often needs help to start flowing. Your conscious mind can provide the assistance. Consciously review your problem before you go to sleep and command your subconscious to work on it. Or issue the same command before any wordless activity—listening to orchestral music, walking, mowing the grass, weeding the garden. The bright idea that comes during the proverbial morning shave or shower is often the result of priming the subconscious before a wordless, familiar act.

"Be silent, and I will teach you wisdom." — Job 33:33

INCONSISTENCY

Lord, permit me an occasional inconsistency because the only completely consistent people are either foolish, weak, unimaginative, or dead.

On a number of recorded occasions, Winston Churchill was drunk. Yet he was one of the world's great leaders.

Abraham Lincoln told dirty jokes. Yet he led the United States in a spiritual crusade against slavery.

In his later years, Henry Ford tolerated thugs to run Ford Motor. Yet he led his company to greatness that lasts to this day.

Samuel Goldwyn's malapropisms—such as "that

makes me so sore it gets my dandruff up" and "in two words: im possible," etc.—are notorious. Yet he led the film industry in some of its greatest creative and economic successes.

Leaders—and everyone else—are inconsistent; they will not succeed at everything. What's more, leaders can't always lead or can't lead in everything. Churchill superbly led his nation in war, but failed after peace was achieved. Lincoln failed in running a store. Ford naively thought he could stop World War I, but failed. Goldwyn produced *Cleopatra,* starring Elizabeth Taylor, an artistic and financial flop.

The best way to lead is to act on the advice we give to others. One outstanding success can often cover a multitude of inconsistencies.

INNOVATION

Lord, let me be daring, be first, be different.

I define innovation as purposeful, organized, risk-taking introduced to maximize opportunities. Generating and introducing new elements gives activities new dimensions.

Innovative ability is conceptual rather than technical or scientific. It is the ability to look at our activities as a system and to think of new concepts or ideas that will change or rearrange our activities into a new and more productive whole.

Innovation occurs primarily in two forms: (a) exploration and improvement within the various parameters of an activity; and (b) the questioning, testing, and establishing of the parameters themselves. In relation to the other central tasks of managing, innovation transcends—and should be a part of—them all.

Innovation cannot be taught in a classroom. Innovation is a state of mind—an openness, a readiness to do something different, a willingness to accept risk and to risk being unaccepted.

Christ was innovative. He did the unexpected. He challenged the religious leaders of his day; he did not keep the Sabbath according to Jewish custom; he taught his followers to love their enemies and to do good to those who hated them; he socialized with sinners; he taught in parables and paradoxes; he told his followers they must submit to be free and die to live.

Lord, make me a true conservative who knows what to conserve.

One definition of a conservative is a person who conserves the good, rejects the bad, and knows which is which. Peter Drucker, the management analyst and author, takes a less sardonic view: "The only means of conservation is innovation."

The need for creativity in business is steadily increasing, he points out, estimating that the demands on the creative abilities of managers have doubled in every generation. A major reason for American economic leadership, he believes, is not the popularly accepted capital formation—in many European and Japanese industries it equals or exceeds that in the United

States—but the higher use in the U. S. of creative managers. For every one hundred dollars spent for direct labor in 1900, the typical American manufacturer spent five to eight dollars for managerial, technical, and professional personnel. Today more is spent on the latter than the former.

Many individuals display one of three self-defeating attitudes toward innovation: (1) they dismiss it as pretentious nonsense; (2) they employ a faddist approach, relying on the superficial use of currently popular programs such as Quality Circles; or (3) they scarcely think about it at all.

The third is the most common and most dangerous attitude. Many managers don't consider themselves creative. Because they wish they were, they shut the painful subject from their minds. In so doing, however, they may stifle the creativity they do possess.

Even the most prosaic individuals have the spark of creativity in their make-up. The manager of an accounting department first suspected such a spark in one of his dullest clerks upon discovering the latter's interest in fine printing. The clerk had a small press in his basement at home on which he turned out superb work. The manager had the clerk transferred to the company's small printing operation where he blossomed, developing several cost-saving ideas and improving the quality of the printing as well. The clerk showed creativity of a high order—but in printing, not accounting.

Everyone needs to find his or her creative niche, then take a positive approach toward practicing conservation (or innovation). When the manager transferred the clerk to the printing operation, he jolted him out of a rut and moved him into an environment where he could perform more creatively.

The average individual probably works at less than fifteen percent of his or her creative potential. Consequently, the doubling of creative effort in every generation lies within the realm of possibility. We are aided by an ever-increasing creative capital—our fund of knowledge and experience—on which to draw for new innovation and conservation.

INSIGHTS

Lord, open my mind to new and fresh insights and make me willing to work hard to get them.

We generally get new insights by accidental discovery, experience, imports, and systematic observation and analysis.

We must rely increasingly on the last technique. *Accident* is too haphazard and infrequent. We are living in such a tumultuous period of change that *experience* is no longer as reliable as in the past. And *imports* help some, but not enough.

In *systematic observation and analysis,* we can markedly increase our insights by taking the following steps:

1. **Train people to do the job.** We train people to perform research in scientific and technological areas. Why not in methods, in organizational development, and in other fields? True, many companies employ methods engineers, but these people usually confine themselves to new methods for using machinery or equipment. Needed are experts who can perform in a range that goes

beyond conventional time and motion study—in office procedures, employee relations, marketing, etc.

2. **Provide observation-and-analysis people with special facilities.** Like scientists, these experts may merit a laboratory or comparable support, just as the scientist does. With the aid of a small staff, a company psychologist performed motivation research in a southern textile plant and learned that hourly employees improved their output with increased responsibility. A group of twenty skilled employees was offered responsibility for all the planning, scheduling, and control functions. When they needed help, they could call on the foreman or any of the other people who had performed those functions. Leadership arose from within the group. One result: a thirty-three percent savings in overhead.

3. **Give specialists access to special information.** This is advisable for the same reason you provide them with special facilities. Researchers for the Encyclopedia Britannica's marketing department asked themselves which non-English-speaking nations in the world had high proportions of people who could read English. The answer: several Western European nations and Japan. Various considerations, including xenophobia, ruled out a strong sales effort for the English-language Britannica in Western Europe, but not in Japan. In one recent year, Britannica sold more English-language sets in Japan than in Great Britain.

4. **Detach the function from day-to-day operations.** Just as you detach the lab from other activities in technology it is important to detach day-to-day operations from the specialists who are analyzing it. The southern textile mill didn't begin to receive substantial benefits from its psychologist until it detached him from the employee-relations activity and gave him a small staff of his own.

> My son, if you accept my words and store up my commands within you, turning your ear to wisdom and applying your heart to understanding, and if you call out for insight and cry aloud for understanding . . . then you will understand the fear of the Lord and find the knowledge of God.
> — Proverbs 2:1–5

INTERRUPTIONS

Lord, let them interrupt me—but not yet.

No one enjoys being interrupted, and many unwelcome intrusions can be forestalled with a little planning and a lot of tact. Yet all the planning and tact we can muster won't forestall all of them. Interruptions are inevitable, and so we must learn how to avoid them whenever possible, but handle them tactfully and efficiently whenever they are unavoidable.

Interruptions fall into two basic categories: internal and external. The following five external distractions will likely be the ones that plague you most often:

Noise. Workmen begin adjusting the air conditioning; loud talk erupts in the corridor; the ballast in the fluorescent lighting goes bad and makes a buzzing sound. These and many other noise distractions can interrupt even the most intense discussion. You can tell the air conditioning people to come back later; you can shoo away the corridor talkers; you can find another place for discussion if the ballast noise is intolerable. The important thing is to do something promptly and with good humor.

The telephone. Although the phone is indispensable, it can also be an interrupter. Instruct your secretary to take calls for the duration. If you have no secretary, attach a gadget to the phone so you can turn it off. The phone is your servant, not vice versa. Whenever possible, pick a meeting room without a telephone; the phone is a common villain because many who would never interrupt in person will interrupt by phone.

Visits from outsiders. The person who wants "just a second of your time"—he doesn't say anything but waits with obvious impatience half in and half out of your office; or the secretary who tiptoes in with a message on a folded slip of paper. Deal with such interruptions firmly, but good humoredly. If possible, station a secretary in a nearby room and instruct her ahead of time to head off unexpected visitors.

The in-and-outer. If you're holding a discussion with only one or two others and one of them gets a visit or a phone call that he or she cannot put off until later, reschedule the meeting. You should, however, let participants know in advance that their cooperation in minimizing interruptions is expected.

The coffee or Coke break. In reasonably short sessions, why stop for beverages? Are you meeting in the desert? If the meeting will be long, a break makes sense; not otherwise. If a break is necessary, plan to have it at a natural transition period, not at some arbitrarily set time.

The preceding suggestions will minimize external distractions, but internal distractions—those caused by someone's action or lack of action—can be the most troublesome:

The uneasy silence. If you and your colleagues suddenly dry up, no one should worry. This happens occasionally in every gathering. Let the silence continue. If there are just two of you, it is best to agree that nothing more needs to be said on the subject. People who cannot endure silence are likely to say the first thing that pops into their heads; and usually it's either irrelevant or repetitious.

Weariness. Learn to recognize signs of fatigue or boredom—that glazed look, repetition, sidebar discussions. To perk up the pace, use some humor or tell of a personal experience that illustrates the point.

The problem participant. This problem can occur whether two or a dozen people are in a discussion. You must deal with this troublemaker immediately, but fairly. Humor can help. The Swedish supervisor in the GE lamp plant would say to the problem person: "Don't interrupt me while I'm interrupting you."

Agenda trouble. Getting off the track is another common internal interruption. In meetings, the lack of an agenda or failure to follow the one you have may be the cause. In a more casual setting, frequent digressions by one or more of your colleagues may generate irritation so extreme in an on-track participant that he or she walks out.

Poor route and mileage markers. This will result if you have agenda trouble, but it can arise even when you know what you want to talk about. In a complex discussion, participants need periodic score-keeping, or some will repeat themselves or grow so frustrated they will wander into irrelevant discussion.

Interruptions and distractions can be a nuisance, but we must always be sensitive when others feel they need us for one reason or another. Jesus was never impatient with those who interrupted him. He always stopped and met their needs without feeling resentment or annoyance.

> While he was saying this, a ruler came and knelt before him and said, "My daughter has just died. But come and put your hand on her, and she will live." Jesus got up and went with him, and so did his disciples. — Matthew 9:18–19

Lord, keep me from interrupting others.

Have you ever considered that you may be guilty of causing most of the interruptions and distractions in meetings involving your employees? For example, do you:

- Add corroborative details to a subordinate's report, throwing the person off pace?

- Break in on others' meetings, forgetting how much you resent it when your boss interrupts *your* session?

- Accept all phone calls during a meeting because one of them might be important?

- Grow impatient with your assistant's detail-mindedness and cut the conversation short?

If you cause these or other interruptions, think about other ways to add the corroborative details to a report or subordinates' meeting. You can always return a phone call and later deal in private with an assistant's over-concern for detail.

Self-discipline is the remedy. When you see the abstracted look in others' eyes, when all conversation stops if you appear, when you tout your open-door policy but few take advantage of it—perhaps you are interrupting too much.

JOB DESCRIPTIONS

Lord, let me define a job so that it can further my organization's goals the most effectively.

The well-written job description contains short, factual statements that minimize the need for interpretation. The use of a standardized glossary is also effective to close communication gaps.

Here's a suggested format for a job description:

1. Identify the job by a meaningful title that reflects duties and responsibilities.
2. State the job's geographic location and organizational unit.
3. Indicate the job's level by identifying the position to which it reports and the positions it supervises.
4. Note the job's purpose and duties, summarized in two or three brief sentences.
5. List the job's major duties and responsibilities.
6. Indicate the job's scope (production or sales volume, etc., for which the position is responsible).

Job descriptions must be honest to be effective. Integrity usually falls short because of sloth, not willful dishonesty. The narration fails to keep pace with developments. Normally, the job description becomes outdated because of changes in the position's scope or reporting relationships.

JOB-HUNTING

Lord, let me see the whole picture, not guess at it from the parts.

George didn't like his manufacturing job with an appliance manufacturer. He wished to return to his real love, engineering, but he didn't want to leave the company and he didn't want to foul the relationship with his boss.

George passed the word of his dissatisfaction to a couple of friends in the organization who he knew were discreet and hoped for something to happen. Nothing did. When he learned that somebody else had won a promotion to a newly created position in engineering, he visited the engineering manager who didn't know he was available. George's emissaries had been too discreet. They had done nothing to help. When George had emphasized discretion, they had taken that as an excuse for inaction. Job searching is rarely easy, and few people do it without powerful motivation—for example, because they need a new spot for themselves.

If you want a better job, the first thing to do is to let key people know you're looking. This is particularly important if you wish to remain with your present employer. When you don't do this, you guess at the whole from the parts.

George should have made his desire known—to his boss first. Little job-hopping onus is attached to those who move fairly often, provided they remain in the family.

Sidney, in contrast, made a point of telling every new

boss early in their association that he sought promotions, preferably in the new manager's component, but elsewhere if that failed. No one resented his direct approach, although a few were surprised.

Sid also confides, "I use the old-boy network. As I get exposure, more people, particularly my present manager and former bosses, know what I can do. When an opening comes up, they'll think of me. I 'sell' to managers only—people in a position to hire others. It's largely a waste of time to have non-managers 'looking' for you." Sid advises: "Tell your present boss about your ambitions. He or she will probably find out anyhow, and your honesty may help minimize the annoyance your boss would feel at learning of them indirectly."

More people move these days. A survey of one thousand business executives revealed that one-third of them occupied jobs that hadn't existed before. A Labor Department study showed that 71 million people in the United States labor force held jobs for an average of 4.2 years compared to 4.6 years only three years earlier.

Another Labor Department survey shows that a person in his or her early twenties can expect to change jobs six or seven times during a lifetime. Instead of thinking of a career, people are thinking of serial careers. And you need far more and far better information under those circumstances.

George tackled the challenge too diffidently, too obliquely. When you seek a better job, either with your present employer or another, mount a vigorous and frontal attack—first to know what's available and second to assure that your availability is known.

Aside from friends in the old-boy network, the best

source on job information appears to be help-wanted ads in publications serving your line of work, in metropolitan newspapers, and in the *Wall Street Journal* or its weekly supplement. Professional recruiting firms offer this service, but they receive mixed reviews from people who have used them to hunt for managerial jobs. One reason lies in the fact that most of them are retained by the employer, not the potential employee. If you happen to have registered with a recruiter who is looking for precisely your qualifications, fine. But that perfect mesh doesn't happen often. Usually a recruiter goes after someone already employed in a job similar to one he is trying to fill.

George finally got a lead on a job by answering a blind ad in the *Wall Street Journal*. When he learned the potential employer was a rival appliance maker, he remembered a college friend, Irving, who worked there. This time he used the old-boy network effectively. Irving assembled information in four areas vital to George: the job's potential, its possible pitfalls, political crosscurrents that could affect it, and George's chances of getting the position.

The first three informational categories, with either the same employer or a potential new one, will help determine whether to pursue the opportunity. The fourth category is vital for fine-tuning an applicant's aggressiveness in seeking the job. In addition, you must evaluate your informant's accuracy and judgment.

You need good judgment to evaluate any proposed job, even if the salary is twenty-five percent higher (which is usually the minimum increase to consider for a position with another employer; with the same employer you can consider a job for less of an increase).

Irving reported that the job involved design, installation, and debugging of new equipment. To George, its attractions lay in the creativity required. This also held dangers. The employer couldn't tolerate many errors.

Irving's appraisal of the political crosscurrents seemed reassuring. He would report to the engineering vice president who, at sixty, would be retiring within five years. At forty-five, that possibility attracted George. He won the new job.

Yet alas! He did not foresee another part of the picture. When the engineering vice president retired in two years, the company folded engineering into manufacturing and eliminated the vice presidency. George had to stay in the same position because the better manfacturing/engineering positions went to those with more tenure.

> My son, preserve sound judgment and discernment, do not let them out of your sight; they will be life for you, an ornament to grace your neck. Then you will go on your way in safety, and your foot will not stumble.
> — Proverbs 3:21–23

LABOR UNIONS

Lord, help me treat my employees so well that a labor union is unnecessary.

A plant manager was considering a possible expansion of shipping facilities, but warned his staff to keep the project secret until he decided to go ahead.

The hint that something was brewing leaked out, but not through the warehouse superintendent. He answered all queries by saying, "I'll let you know when the time is right."

Nor did a supervisor reveal the secret. He just looked mysterious and spoke vaguely of the need to keep modern and have the latest in facilities.

Within a week, rumors raged throughout the plant. Most credence went to those originating among the supervisor's people. His references to keeping modern and having the latest in facilities gave apparent support to the grapevine report that a computer was on order. The warehouse personnel became convinced that the computer was destined for their operation and would eliminate jobs. Strangers had looked over their area recently and were probably representatives of a computer manufacturer. (Actually, they were engineers from a construction firm, studying the proposed expansion of shipping facilities.)

The storm got back to the plant manager who hastily revealed the project expansion. But he was too late. Many employees didn't think the matter could be that prosaic. They invited a union representative to talk to them. Even when the plant manager did expand the shipping area, the unionization drive had already taken on a life of its own.

The episode reveals three axioms about interpersonal relationships:

1. Everything you do or don't do communicates something. It's impossible not to communicate. By his secrecy, the plant manager thought he was not communicating, but he was—the wrong message.

2. Because you communicate constantly, you have to

watch yourself constantly to do it positively and to do it right. Even though committed—mistakenly—to secrecy, the warehouse superintendent could have relieved the flatness of his "I'll let you know when the time is right." He could have said, "I can't tell you now, but when the time is right, it will be good news for you."

3. Whoever communicates the most effectively will precipitate the action. In this case the supervisor communicated the most effectively, even though unwittingly, and the action his message precipitated was a visit from a union representative.

Much to the manager's dismay, the union won the representation election. The plant manager thought he had been avoiding misunderstanding by not communicating—in the warehouse expansion case as well as in many other instances—but instead he had been allowing misinformation to surface by keeping silent.

Lord, if there is to be a union here, let my relations with it be positive.

The basic relationship between a company and a labor union is made up of many complex variables built on past practice. The relationship brings together individuals and groups with different backgrounds, points of view, interests, and strengths. The balance of power is almost never equal; one party is usually dominant. These relative strengths vary from time to time and situation to situation.

It is important, therefore, to establish, implement, and maintain a rational and objective approach for dealing with the union—one that considers both parties' needs and interests.

When business problems occur the blame most often is placed on "deteriorating relations with the union," with each side pointing the finger at the other. However, serious business problems resulting from labor strife and restrictive union practices are in many cases just as much the fault of management as of the union.

Unions can only make demands or try to take control. Therefore, professional managers must provide regular, careful, and critical attention to the labor relations climate.

Labor relations decisions should be based on research and planning, just as is done with a new product concept before designing, manufacturing, and marketing it. Labor unions spend the necessary funds to research today's problems, as well as to plan for the future. Management must do the same.

Regularly ask yourself these questions: Is labor relations a mainstream operating activity in my organization? Is the activity properly staffed? Are the people responsible held accountable for significant results? Do they know where the business is going?

LEADERSHIP

Lord, give me sight to lead so that my employees and I do not fall into the ditch.

Good leadership requires that appropriate relationships be established with subordinates before anything else is done. The manager's credibility and potential effectiveness stem from this relationship.

According to studies of relationships between leaders and subordinates, the key behavioral characteristics of managers include flexibility, display of trust, susceptibility to influence from others, and behavior that goes beyond basic contractual relations. This last point chiefly means that the leader and subordinate have give and take between them, with the understanding that constraints will not limit reasonable and responsible goal-directed behavior.

When Jesus' disciples uneasily told him that he was offending the Pharisees, Jesus replied: "Leave them; they are blind guides. If a blind man leads a blind man, both will fall into the pit" (Matthew 15:14). When Peter still had reservations about Jesus' attitude, Christ answered in a rare burst of exasperation, "Are you still so dull?" Jesus knew that leadership required clear vision and that the Pharisees could only see behind them; they were looking to the past and ignoring the future.

LOYALTY

Lord, keep me loyal to worthy people and goals even if I may not wholly like either.

> If I'm loyal alone
>   To those I admire
> And to objectives
>   That set my soul afire,
> How deal I with men
>   Just a bit aloof
> And those many goals
>   That seem fireproof?

> The answer, not
> > Lost in the fog,
> Lies plain as a match
> > At the hearth log:
> Christ's Golden Rule
> > Sets me alight
> So people help me
> > Make dull goals bright.
>
> — John S. Morgan

MANAGERIAL STYLE

Lord, help me see the strengths and weaknesses of my employees and manage them in a way that will enhance their strengths and minimize their weaknesses.

Cal's resume was impressive. After graduating from Northwestern with a journalism degree, he went to work for a Chicago-based trade magazine. Within two years he moved to New York to work for a consumer magazine. He left that post three years later to join a land development company. That ended after only eighteen months because of "an offer too good to pass up to rejoin the consumer magazine as managing editor." But that publication changed ownership within two years, and Cal "chose not to accept the new owner's employment offer." Instead he decided to "realize a long-held ambition to go into business for myself as a consultant to housing supply manufacturers and home builders." With seeming candor, the resume acknowledged that the consulting business failed "because of the bankruptcy of a major client."

The vice president who was interviewing Cal was intrigued by him. At 32, he had just the right background for a sales promotion professional. Even his salary request, $35,000 annually, was in line. Yet alarm bells rang. The money demand was *too* reasonable. Cal had job-hopped too much. Instead of making an offer, the vice president made a few phone calls, none to the references listed.

He learned that Cal had not exactly lied in his job interview and resume, but neither had he told the full truth. He was asked to leave, but not fired from, the Chicago magazine because of his discordant personality. He was asked to leave the New York publication for the same reason. Although he returned to it, he did so because the land development job proved a dead end and the consumer publication had heavy staff turnover. He left because the new owner declined to continue him as managing editor. In his consulting business, his major client did indeed go bankrupt, but Cal knew of its poor health when he took it on.

The vice president offered Cal a job at $32,000 a year. He chose that figure because his budget permitted it and because he learned that Cal had earned less than half that the previous year in his own business. And he offered the job with strings. He tied the proposal with advice and a proviso. He didn't tell Cal he had learned some facts disputing his resume claims. Instead he flatly told him that he was too ambitious and that this trait had led him into numerous job changes and into some bad decisions in his consulting work.

"You're going to be on your own here, but responsible

to me," he told Cal. "The sales promotion staff will consist of you and a secretary—no one else. The advertising and employee communication work is performed by others. When you want legitimate sales promotion work done by either department, you work through me. The first sign that you are stirring up discord in my staff means your automatic dismissal."

Cal started to protest, but the communications vice president interrupted. "I know this sounds tough, and I don't normally lay down rules like these. But I believe you're a special case. You're a gifted guy, but you haven't realized anywhere near your potential. You've frittered away your opportunities thus far. I'm giving you a chance to make something of yourself—and to help me, of course. I believe this is the only way we both can achieve what we want."

Cal took the job. Although he went through some difficult times with the vice president, he came to recognize that joining him was the best thing for his career; he became the premier sales promotion professional in his field.

The vice president started Cal on the right foot. First, he isolated him from the rest of his staff to guard against organizational chaos. Second, he managed him with a firmer hand than he did other staff members because he was error-prone. Third, he praised him lavishly for the many examples of good work he did. Fourth, he upgraded his job title from time to time—from specialist to consultant to manager for sales promotion.

Cal was fortunate to have a strong and wise manager who channeled his ambitions constructively.

> The wise in heart accept commands, but a chattering fool comes to ruin.
> — Proverbs 10:8

Lord, help me simplify, because therein lies the secret of good management.

For years, advocates have urged simplification as a means to improve everything from management, to art, to living itself. In management, the guidelines for simplification are these:

- Organize the facts of the work for examination with analytical techniques, charts, and diagrams.

- Carefully review each step of procedures and eliminate waste of any kind, such as in time, energy, space, material, and equipment.

- Reorganize the procedure.

Underpinning these three steps are the following considerations:
1. Concentrate on one project at a time, not on all management tasks—nor on all of art or living.
2. Rely on the common sense, expertise, and understanding of everyone involved in the work—even indirectly.

Lord, keep me from creating a homogenized environment; I want the cream to rise.

A dictionary definition of homogenized is "of a similar

structure, as in a culture." One style of homogenized environment is caused by cautious managers, who, when confronted with a new idea, respond in one or more of the following ways:

- Drag their feet. Who can argue with painstaking bosses who want to "run it through once more"?

- Say yes but mean no. Their diplomacy leaves almost everyone pleased—for a while.

- Wait for full analysis. Logic and management texts seem to be on their side.

- Don't follow up—just drop the idea among employees and let them worry about it (sometimes this is mistakenly called "Bottoms Up Management").

- Call meetings—lots of them. They will kill both time and interest in the idea.

- Put it into channels. It will make the rounds and return three months later with seventeen sets of initials. Unfortunately, the first were those of Fred Y. Ingram, misleading every subsequent reader into thinking it was merely a "for your information" memo.

- Boost the cost estimates. This will almost guarantee a veto of the idea.

- Worry about the budget. This is especially effective when used with boosted cost estimates, but it can stand alone in blocking any idea.

- Wait for market surveys. This reduces the possibility of mistakes—and of positive moves.

- Stick to protocol. Hypersensitive feelings of fellow employees will be around long after a dead idea.

- Cultivate the NIH syndrome. If it was "not invented here" or if it's some outsider's idea, cautious managers won't push it because "we pride ourselves on being a self-generating organization."

You, of course, would not be guilty of these sins. Or, would you? There is logic in some of them—wait for a full analysis and market survey, be concerned about costs and budgets, and let the idea simmer. Within reason, you should do all these things to get the cream of the ideas. The key is not to overdo in any of these areas.

Over-simmering has probably ruined more good ideas than any other factor because *some* simmering—sometimes called idea incubation—is absolutely necessary to get the cream to the top.

Matthew Arnold, the nineteenth-century English writer and critic, advised: "Let us think of quietly enlarging our stock of true and fresh ideas, and not, as soon as we get an idea or half an idea, be running out with it into the street, and trying to make it rule there. Our ideas will, in the end, shape the world better for maturing a little."

Here are suggestions on how to avoid over-simmering:

- Let the idea sit in your notebook, on tape, or in the lab for at least a few days, but not for much more than a week. Then come back to it to see if it still looks as good.

- Ask yourself questions about the idea. If it's a product idea, for example, can you increase its function by making it do more things? Can you get higher performance by making it last longer, be safer or easier to repair? Can you lower its cost? Can you increase its salability by improving its appearance, distribution, and so on?

- Distinguish between merely fussing with and really improving an idea. Endless tinkering may lead to senility, not maturity in your innovation.

- Accept constructive suggestions.

- Evaluate the idea as to how much trouble it would cause. Some ideas would cost too much to put into effect, or take too long to implement, or cause too much upset among employees.

When you have simmered the milk of your idea properly, the cream will naturally rise. Do it improperly and you will have an homogenized result, with the idea blended and lost.

> Whoever watches the wind will not plant; whoever looks at the clouds will not reap. — Ecclesiastes 11:4

MONEY

Lord, make money always my excellent servant, never my terrible master.

Ken and Bert were hired in the same year and both started in the bank's public relations department. Within a year, Ken became the department manager, married, and bought a house.

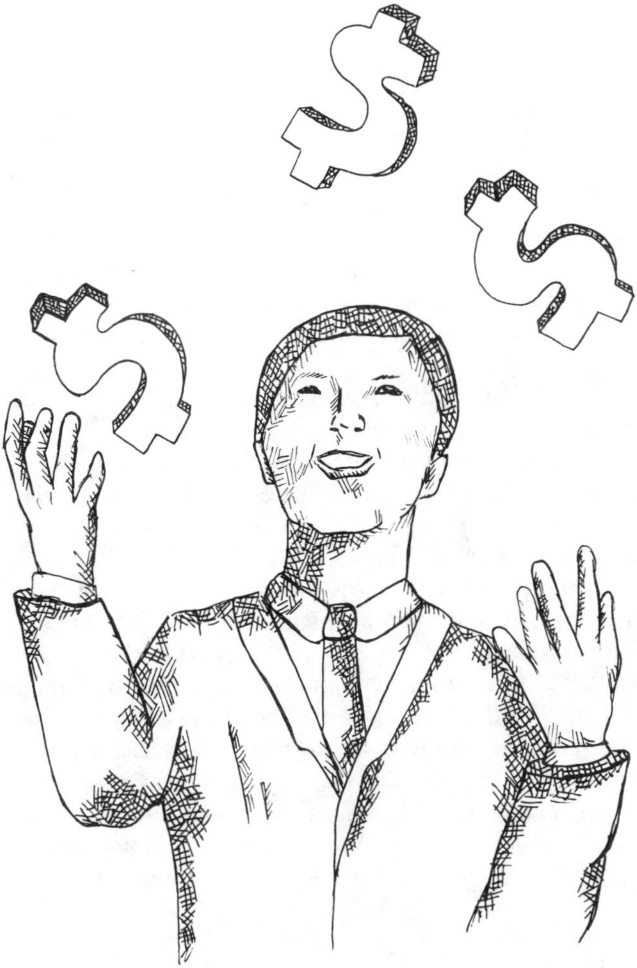

Bert too married, but he and his new wife stayed in his rented apartment. His wife also worked for the bank and the couple participated in their employer's savings plan whereby the bank matched fifty cents of every dollar they saved up to six percent of their combined salaries.

Ken had started in the savings plan, but had to withdraw to meet mortgage payments on his house. His wife quit her bank position soon after they married when she discovered she was pregnant. To make ends meet, Ken hunted for a higher paying job with a PR agency. He found one because he persuaded the bank to use a certain agency to supplement its inside department. He went to that agency.

Bert became manager of the smaller inside unit when Ken left, winning a modest increase in salary.

At first Ken prospered handsomely at the agency, bought a second car for his wife, a cottage on a nearby lake, and a boat to go with the cottage. Soon, however, he realized he had overextended himself. Convinced that he could make more in his own agency, he formed one. Yet the bank didn't go with him to the new venture as he had expected. In fact, Bert persuaded his boss that the bank would save money and get a more effective job if it returned to doing its own public relations. He was right and was rewarded with a good salary increase.

In the meantime, Ken had trouble as an entrepreneur. Two small clients left him, a third went bankrupt owing him a substantial sum of money. Ken's young firm soon followed into dissolution. Money troubles soured his marriage, and his wife divorced him. He gave up the cottage and boat. His wife got the house.

Bert continued to run the bank's public relations and used part of his money from the savings plan to get started with a house. His wife took maternity leave from the bank, but planned to return to work.

Ken tried to return as a hired hand in some agency, but none would have him because of his reputation for pirating others' accounts. He finally landed a job as a press agent for the city's professional tennis team. To show for the three years since he had left the bank, he had a divorce, an ulcer, and a job paying less than when he started in the field.

Bert had a good marriage, a baby on the way, a home, and a steadily improving job because the bank acquired three smaller financial institutions and he headed public relations for all of his employer's expanding business.

Bert let money work for him; Ken worked for money.

> Dishonest money dwindles away, but he who gathers money little by little makes it grow. — Proverbs 13:11

MOTIVATION

Lord, help me motivate people to work better together, but not necessarily harder.

Experts generally agree that human input, equipment, facility layout, product or service design, and percentage of capacity used are the five most important factors contributing to productivity. Dramatic improvements in productivity occur with concentrated effort in just one of these areas.

Let's focus on an area that does not cost a dime or involve any reorganization or other steps requiring consultation or approval: the human element, which accounts for as much as eighty percent of productivity in some cases, and rarely less than ten percent.

If you motivate employees to work better together (but not necessarily harder) you can accomplish miracles. That's the secret behind such formalized motivational plans as Scanlon, Rucker, and many others. You can develop your own plan on this framework:

1. **Make the facts of work and work relationships serve you.** Motivation is a team proposition. If you stimulate one employee, he or she will help you convince the next.

2. **Let employees know how you feel about the job.** They need to see your positive attitude. Men sometimes have more difficulty with this than women, a reason why women often make better managers than men. Examine your feelings about the job as well. If you feel cynical, listless, or doubtful about its value or importance, those emotions will probably infect your employees. Cynicism and related maladies deaden other emotions, making positive motivation more difficult.

3. **Talk up, not down, to employees.** Condescension is fatal. Talking down deadens initiative; it implies the listener is a simpleton or not worth talking to on an equal level.

4. **Watch out for paternal attitudes.** These are related to condescension and probably much more common than naked dictatorship. You cannot buy loyalty with promises of protection or favors, which is what paternalism tries to do.

5. **Hear others' viewpoints.** No one knows all the answers.

6. **Build the motivational climate carefully.** An abrupt change in managerial style, for example, will breed

suspicion. Change gradually, as the circumstances call for it. For instance, when a discipline problem comes up, if you formerly handled such things in public, handle it in private and resolve to do so from then on.

7. **Communicate better.** Communicate as continuously as possible, deal with both big and little matters with equal care, be concrete and specific, acknowledge difficulties, show how you propose to deal with trouble, know your audience and purpose, think and organize, guard your credibility and act on what you say.

8. **Be ready for emergencies.** When you deal with people, you must expect the unexpected. Remain patient, keep cool—and have a prayer handy.

OBSERVATION

Lord, develop my powers of observation, the essence of originality.

Why have artists frequently been great inventors also? Leonardo da Vinci is the outstanding example. Besides his paintings and sculpture, he conceived all manner of inventions, including the scissors. Alexander Graham Bell was a painter before he conceived the "talking wire" or telephone. Other examples are Samuel F. B. Morse, inventor of the telegraph, and Robert Fulton, creator of the first commercially successful steamboat. Both began as portrait painters. Two politically creative men, Winston Churchill and Dwight D. Eisenhower, were gifted amateur painters.

Artists must exercise keen observation to be good at what they do. Their skill in observing may be applied with equal success to other creative fields because the same fundamental ability underlies all innovation.

Managers as well as artists can develop powers of observation by practicing—by observing. Here are exercises to help. The first will limber us up.

1. **Look at people.** When you are on a plane, train, bus, in a long queue, or whenever you have time to observe other people, try to guess their occupations by their mannerisms, appearance, etc.

In the second exercise, we observe as a realtor might.

2. **Examine a building.** What is its architectural style—or does it incorporate several styles? What materials have gone into its construction? What other buildings does it remind you of? To what additional purpose could the building be put?

In the third exercise, we see how to develop a creative idea by taking an attribute of a household appliance and applying it to a different use, a possible home workshop tool.

3. **Examine a small household appliance, the electric mixer.** What's it made of? What noncooking use can you think of for it? Will it mix paint? How could it be adapted for such uses? Can you buy such a device now in the hardware store? If not, would a market exist for it? How can you find out?

Exercise four is from an actual creative adventure. A man working for the municipal bus company created a weekly mystery tour program from an idea that sprang from Sunday afternoon drives with his family. The bus firm sought a way to better utilize its expensive equipment, much of which stood idle on Sundays. For a modest price, the bus company offered a six-hour tour every Sunday, with stops at unannounced points of interest.

4. **Take a Sunday drive with no fixed destination.** Be alert for road markers that inform the public, "one mile to George Washington's Winter Headquarters," or "Makepeace Lovett's Homestead, Next Right." Visit several such places of interest. When are they open? Are they interesting? How long does it take to go through them? Is an admission fee charged? How many people can the place accommodate at one time? Do they welcome parties of thirty to forty people? Could a bus company run tours to a few of these spots in four to six hours?

As you observe attributes for possible ideas, test them against the following checklist to determine, first, if you have actually observed attributes that might engender an idea, and, second, if you can apply the idea to an actual situation. To demonstrate, let's assume you observe the mixing attribute of a kitchen appliance and want to convert it to a paint mixer:

1. **Does the attribute have commercial possibilities?** Yes, it might serve as a workshop tool to be sold in hardware stores.

2. **Does the attribute offer labor-saving possibilities?** Yes, it can relieve the wearying chore of mixing.

3. **Could the attribute preserve health or well-being?** Yes, perhaps it could be adapted to a whirlpool bath.

4. **Could the attribute appeal to beauty or the senses?** Yes, the workshop mixer could have an attractive physical design.

5. **Is the attribute compatible with current technology?** Yes, it is technologically practical and ties in with the current do-it-yourself trend.

Creativity often requires us to come up with a series of observed attributes that we meld and weld into a new product, method, or system for doing a job. The automobile as we now know it is an example. Originally, it was a simple machine, little more than a motorized buggy. It has developed into a juggernaut, with automatic transmission, high speed and power assists for steering, braking, and moving windows. Attributes observed elsewhere were adapted to the auto.

Adaptations of observed attributes may occur in one or more different ways. For instance, they may occur as the result of:

■ **A discovery**—a first-time perception of something hitherto unknown. Galileo's theory that the earth revolves around the sun was a discovery.

■ **An innovation**—a new or novel element applied to an existing way of doing something. The auto was an innovative kind of creation—it substituted mechanical power for animal power.

■ **A synthesis**—a different mixture of known elements or parts to make a new whole. The airplane is an example here. The internal combustion engine had been developed in the eighteenth century. Experiments with gliders had occurred in the early nineteenth century. In the early twentieth century, the Wright brothers combined the gasoline internal combustion engine with the glider and produced an entirely new means of transportation.

■ **A mutation**—an alteration in the form or qualities of an existing entity or concept. This has occurred in agriculture. Today's hybrid corn, for instance, is a mutation of the original corn planted by the American Indians.

Observation lies at the base of all this. When we fully develop our powers of observation we will unlock the closet doors of ideas. And the more ideas we have, the more likely that some of them will be good.

> Sow your seed in the morning, and at evening let not your hands be idle, for you do not know which will succeed, whether this or that, or whether both will do equally well.
> — Ecclesiastes 11:6

OPEN-MINDEDNESS

Lord, never let me close up my mind.

Decades ago, nearly all machinery in the United States was black. Why? For no real reason, except that it had always been that way. A manager for a New England shoe manufacturer noticed that one of his veteran employees had trouble with his eyes and, consequently, with his production. The black leather and the black machinery offered too little contrast. The manager ordered the machine painted a contrasting color, but the veteran operator protested: Machinery should be black—a matter of tradition. A different-colored machine in the shop would look funny. The lighter color would show the dirt quicker and would have to be cleaned more often.

The manager prevailed and had the machine painted a light gray. The operator kept grumbling until his mate at the next machine asked for gray too. Then the first operator admitted he could see better, and his output increased measurably. Another operator suggested painting moving parts red for safety's sake. The idea caught on all over the shoe-manufacturing plant, and other manufacturers picked it up. Today, machinery in a variety of hues—usually light green, buff, or gray—is commonplace.

The first operator's initial objections stemmed from a closed mind. The closed mind results from many causes, but these four stand out: 1) need for the familiar; 2) need for excessive order and integration; 3) fear of risk or speculation; 4) compulsion to conform.

Let's examine each in more detail.

1. **Need for the familiar.** The veteran shoe-machine operator required the familiar to support his need for security. He initially resisted an improvement, even though it promised—and eventually delivered—benefits to him. Before you dismiss him as an exceptionally reactionary case, ask yourself these questions: Did the last suit you bought match or nearly match one you already owned? Do you resist your spouse's suggestions to move the furniture? Do you honestly welcome changed routines at work? Do you ever suggest such changes yourself? Do you ever challenge seemingly meaningless practices at work? Do you genuinely welcome a new employee at work?

If you honestly must answer no to three or more of these six questions, you have strong needs for the familiar yourself. Many of us build a comfortable little rut in which to operate—one that we can take for granted and that satisfies our need for stability and security.

What can you do about inertia, habits that are too comfortable, laziness, and advancing age, all of which solidify us into familiar thought and work patterns? Here are suggestions:

First, be aware of the danger. Recognize the natural human tendency to cling to the familiar. When confronted with a fresh idea, always ask yourself, "Do I resist this because it's new?"

Second, break habit patterns from time to time. Do this just to stir the blood. Initially, switch some morning routine—brush your teeth after breakfast instead of before, or vice versa. Then, look at some of your work routines and change any that might be improved.

Third, turn inertia to a positive use. Once you get moving out of habit patterns, inertia can keep you moving out of them.

Fourth, put laziness to work. Man invented the wheel because he didn't want to use his own legs and back so much. Many great inventions and developments came along to take some of the work out of work. Fortunately, man's aversion to hard physical effort or tedium is stronger than his need for the familiar.

2. **Need for excessive order and integration.** We also call this problem "hardening of the categories"—a disease common in structured settings that accept only information that easily fits existing classifications. Individuals with this malady tend to react defensively and reject ideas and information for which they have no ready-made slots.

What can you do to overcome the need for excessive order and integration? The remedies for combating the need for the familiar apply here, too, plus these additional prescriptions:

First, try new kinds of order. Vary your morning routines. Second, try disorder occasionally. Skip morning routines altogether for a while. Third, be aware of your tendency toward excessive order. Fourth, think positively. This helps at any time, but it works especially well to overcome excessive order and to keep from relying too much on the familiar. Don't try this suggestion with muscles clenched and mind set in determination to get out of your rut. Instead, simply be conscious that you do not wish to become stifled by excessive order or need for the familiar. The involuntary muscles of your body and the cells of your brain will help you get out of the rut—and without herculean effort of mind or body.

3. **Fear of risk and speculation.** Take to heart the advice that accompanies the prayers on RISK (see pages 220–224).

4. **Compulsion to conform.** The following list of symptoms will help you determine if you suffer from this problem:

- Decisions made largely on the basis of the opinions of others.

- Feelings of self-respect and self-worth based largely on what others think of you.

- Stereotyped ways of acting and thinking.

- A belief that to fit in and belong to a group you must imitate the members and conform to their mindsets.

- Preference for passive observation, not participation.

If you suspect you have conformity troubles, we suggest you:

- Learn from your own and others' mistakes. Analyze past events that went wrong and try to decide why.

- Develop your strengths and learn ways to compensate for weaknesses by observing how others have overcome similar shortcomings.

- Do something out of character occasionally.

- Be prepared. Always have facts and examples to support your case. Present them cautiously, especially when you are in the minority, but not self-consciously. In time the chairperson may assign you the role of devil's advocate or thought-provoker.

ORGANIZATIONS

Lord, remind me that the organization is man's servant, not vice versa.

The larger the organization, the more vulnerable are some of its managers to the "satrap syndrome"—the fallacy that the organization itself is supreme and that the role of its managers is to keep it that way.

An organization is like an erector set, subject to constant modification according to the conditions to which it must be adapted. If an organization does not change with those conditions, it will surely collapse.

There are no precise structural guidelines to follow in setting up an organization. They vary according to local conditions, purposes and policies, available personnel, scale of operations, and diversity or similarity of products or services.

The key to how well any organization works is the people who run it. Competent, dedicated managers can make a Mickey Mouse organization operate well. Incompetent, self-serving managers can run to ruin an organization devised by Peter Drucker.

The organization is mindless. Problems arise when self-serving individuals, perhaps calling themselves "organizational planners," persuade us it can think.

Authors of the Bible knew all about the satrap syndrome, although they didn't call it that. The story in Daniel about Shadrach, Meshach, and Abednego surviving Nebuchadnezzar's fire is a tale of triumphant resistance to "organizational wisdom."

PAPERWORK

Lord, if we can conquer gravity, why do we let paperwork get us down?

Clerical productivity offers a rich opportunity to improve methods because, even with computerization, it is improving at only a fraction of the rate of improvement in manufacturing areas.

In successful improvement programs, the innovator can usually do the job most effectively in this sequence:

1. **Pick the task to improve.** Sometimes this is the most troublesome part of the entire effort. A distributor of industrial supplies decided that slow order fulfillment caused lagging sales. A costly new computerized method replaced the old handwritten process. It speeded

fulfillment, but not incoming orders. It turned out that the problem was an obsolete product line, not order fulfillment.

To choose the most serious paperwork problem, try the following:

- Devise ways to test your decision in advance. Canvass your people. They may know more about the problem than you do.

- Read available literature on the problem. Where has it cropped up before? What did others do about it?

- Seek advice from outsiders in areas where you lack expertise. Mistakes often occur in the area of the innovator's blind spot. If you have had little experience in marketing—a common Achilles heel for innovators—obtain counsel there.

- Review alternate tasks to improve. Apply the foregoing tests to them.

2. **Study the task to improve.** Many innovators slip up here. They do it hurriedly or superficially. A vice president of finance decided he needed better accounting reports. After studying the problem in detail, he was able to eliminate one-third of existing reports—they proved unnecessary or redundant—by revising the remaining two-thirds to give him what the discarded one-third had provided. A superficial job would have resulted in no eliminations and probably greater complexities in all the existing reports.

3. **Challenge everything.** As a result of his study, the finance vice president ordered that all reports be reviewed annually for relevance. At the next review, fifteen percent of the remaining reports were eliminated.

4. **Work out a better way.** The annual restudy decreed by the finance vice president *was* the better way; twelve percent of the remaining reports were cut out in the third annual review. Remember this fundamental truth: if you know what your problem is, if you have studied it, and if you have challenged all established ways of doing things, you usually *can* work out a better way.

5. **Apply the new way.** To fail to apply the new way is analogous to the salesman who doesn't ask for the order.

6. **Follow up.** The audit often constitutes a handy way to follow up—first to find out how the methods changes are working; second to make sure no backsliding has occurred.

> Whoever loves discipline loves knowledge, but he who hates correction is stupid.
> — Proverbs 12:1

PATIENCE

Lord, give me patience—now.

This prayer is not intended to be flippant. Managers must always have patience; when a crisis strikes, they cannot wait until the next day for the patience to handle it.

Controversies among employees are inevitable, and it is the manager's job to settle them. When the parties to a dispute let their feelings become involved, it will grow unpleasant. But we cannot ignore the problem, hoping it will resolve itself. We need everyone working together all the time, because a boat being rowed in two directions at once goes nowhere. We can resolve disputes by exercising patience, using common sense, and remembering these don'ts:

- Don't let disputes get away from you. When one flares up, give it your full attention immediately to resolve it as rapidly as possible. Controversies usually grow worse with time, not better, so don't sit back, hoping they will blow over.

- Never threaten employees or use "or else" tactics. Curb your first impulse to knock heads together. Every dispute has a cause or causes. Find it and make corrections to avoid a recurrence.

- Don't become emotionally involved. That accomplishes nothing except to inflame an already hot situation.

- Don't take sides. Patiently hear all parties, ignoring personalities, and concentrate on issues.

- Don't bruise any egos. If your decision involves removing any responsibility from an employee, try to replace it with something else.

- Don't make decisions that go against the interests of other employees or the organization as a whole.

- Don't ignore the troublesome individuals, among whom most controversies arise. Preventive medicine may forestall ills before they reach the contagious stage.

- Above all, don't lose your good humor and tolerance.

> Hatred stirs up dissension, but love covers over all wrongs.
> — Proverbs 10:12

Lord, grant me humor, understanding, and patience in dealing with difficult people.

Vince surreptitiously looked at his watch—11:30! He had been listening for nearly two hours while the old man raved with complaint after complaint. Now he was carrying on about the diodes they bought from an outside vendor.

"This is the worst junk they've foisted on us yet," he said. "Tell purchasing we won't accept another shipment."

"But Luke," protested his assistant, "we've cleaned that one up already. They've sent replacements, plus profuse apologies."

"Why didn't you stop me before my ticker got in an uproar?" The production manager slammed the offending diode into his wastebasket. "I'm the last to know. Lousy communication."

"I figured you needed a good mad, after the boredom of a vacation." When his boss smiled fleetingly, Vince risked an elaboration. "A memo explains it all. I put it in writing because I know how you love memos. I see it on your back table." Although Vince knew Luke would not read it, he had written it anyway; it would serve as a checklist for himself. He had a copy tucked in his notebook.

"If I read everything that passes across my desk, I'd get nothing else done. That's your job, to free me from paperwork."

"Noted." Vince pretended to write in his book.

"You haven't told me about the new computerized crap."

"Debugging will be finished by the end of this week."

The news didn't seem to cheer the production manager much. "I'll give the word to Owings. He wants to see me this afternoon in one of his blasted meetings that will probably last forever."

Vince kept his face expressionless, saving his best shot for last. "We'll finish the Western Industries job by the end of the second shift and ship tomorrow—two days ahead of schedule."

Luke just grunted, his standard response to good news. Vince escaped from the office before his boss could think of another complaint. In three years as his assistant, he had developed the following defenses against the production manager's onslaughts.

1. He kept his good humor, no matter what the provocation to lose it. Luke could annoy or anger him, but he never let him see it. Hypocritical? No, good self-control.

2. He diagnosed potential trouble spots before they became serious or even difficult or troublesome. This involved constant alertness and being on top of his job.

3. He never blamed others. He was ultimately responsible.

4. He gave the full story. Vince recognized he could forestall many of Luke's complaints by assuring him he need not worry. Vince's competence and honesty had won Luke's trust. But he never knowingly omitted anything. Dishonesties of commission are relatively rare, of omission common.

5. Vince gave advance notice of trouble and triumphs. He had learned, "Never surprise your boss, even pleasantly."

6. Vince watched for the true meanings behind Luke's

outbursts. He understood the psychology that embittered Luke. As a bull of the woods who had climbed from the factory floor to foreman, to general foreman, and finally to production manager, he was a rarity in the company's management. With less formal schooling and polish than any of his peers, he felt defensive.

Late that afternoon, Vince was in his own office reminding himself of his boss's virtues, which he had to do after sessions like the one in the morning. A phone call interrupted him. President Owings wanted to see him. Vince surprised himself by not being surprised when he learned that Luke was taking early retirement and that he, Vince, had been Luke's choice and everyone else's to succeed as production manager.

When he left Owings, Vince rushed back to Luke's office.

"I fooled you this time, didn't I?" chortled his erstwhile boss. He held up his hand to stop Vince's words. "No pieties, boy. I've been thinking of doing this for a long time. I gave Owings my decision this afternoon. I know you'll do a great job. And I know you'll be glad to see the last of me in this chair. No, I want to say this. For at least a year I've been a pain to everyone around me, but most of all to myself. I need to get out of here while I still have a little dignity left. You let me keep some of that dignity, Vince. For a kid, you're quite a guy."

When alone again, the new production manager began planning a retirement party for his friend.

> It is not good to have zeal without knowledge, nor to be hasty and miss the way.
> — Proverbs 19:2

PERSEVERENCE

> Lord, make my efforts known by the name of perseverence rather than obstinacy.

Jim is in prison now—his flamboyant career as head of a high-flying conglomerate was brought to an abrupt halt with his conviction for stock fraud. The accountants, lawyers, and others tried to tell him that he was breaking the law, but he obstinately ignored their counsel.

Among the others who tried to advise him was Albert. But he was only a vice president of the smallest of a score of companies Jim had accquired. Jim sloughed him off, as he did anyone who gave him opinions he did not welcome. After trying twice, Albert concentrated all his energies on keeping his small part of the empire afloat.

Now he has a bigger job—trying to reassemble the more profitable pieces of Jim's ramshackle structure. Following a careful study of Albert's reorganization proposal, the banks extended him a line of credit that he believes will help him rebuild the conglomerate. Although Albert plans this on far more modest lines than Jim's visionary dreams, lawyers, accountants, and bankers will monitor his every move to keep him legally and successfully on the track.

Albert was the oldest remaining executive in the acquired firms. Even though he had disapproved when the family that owned the business sold out to Jim, and even though he had increasingly opposed the conglomerate's approach to business generally, he had persistently refused to leave the company to which he had already devoted twenty-three years of his life. During the two years of Jim's ownership, Albert had fought a holding action, resisting short-sighted moves for quick and high profits. At the crash, Albert's unit was the only one in the entire setup still showing respectable earnings.

Albert is winning through perseverence. Jim lost through stubborness.

> Wicked men are overthrown and are no more, but the house of the righteous stands firm. — Proverbs 12:7

PLANNING

Lord, teach me to use careful planning to reduce idleness and non-productivity.

Idleness and poor productivity have many causes, but one stands out: Lack of planning, especially in the use of available manpower.

Three steps are essential to good manpower planning:

1. **Take stock.** Learn about past productivity rates, employment levels, and turnover rates. Analyze your organization's managerial, technical, and other work forces by experience, age level, and potential.

2. **Make yearly projections.** Use data from step one and project figures one year ahead on the basis of general forecasts. Remember that goals and forecasts must be consistent with your unit's overall goals and objectives.

3. **Use the projection.** The best planning and charts in the world are useless if you don't put them to work.

The following steps will help insure the success of your manpower planning efforts:

1. **Get top management support.** The top manager in your department must fully support the program or it will never be put into action.

2. **Get managerial support at all levels.** When the general manager approves, the next step is to enlist support from all other managerial echelons.

3. **Communicate fully and frequently about manpower planning.** This reassures people and also serves notice that idleness and non-productivity are not in your planning.

4. **Go first class.** This action communicates your commitment to good manpower planning and improves chances for success.

As a manager, you do manpower planning either by design or default. Performed well, manpower planning accomplishes the following:

■ Gives you more flexibility in managing your operation, allowing you to make better use of under-utilized time or talents.

■ Helps you find and keep better employees.

■ Gives your employees a greater sense of accomplishment and stability, making them want to work more efficiently.

When the manpower function is planned, employees themselves are more comfortable. They welcome the sense of purpose and are relieved to know that stability is one of the objectives. Stability can be—indeed, must be—achieved in the midst of the changes going on around us. An unstable environment is a non-productive environment. Planned progress and orderly development of manpower will provide stability even though changes continue.

> Whatever you do, work at it with all your heart.
> — Colossians 3:23

POTENTIAL REALIZATION

Lord, teach me how to learn about myself.

As Cervantes remarked in *Don Quixote,* knowing yourself "is the most difficult lesson in the world."

Adversity is one teacher of the lesson. Charles B. Darrow, a heating engineer, lost his job in 1929. In 1930 he invented the game *Monopoly* and made his own sets for which he charged four dollars. Soon sales mounted to 20,000 a year. In 1935 Darrow sold the game to Parker Brothers. He retired and lived in comfortable retirement until his death in 1967 at the age of 78. Devising games was his true calling.

The attempt to help others can also teach. Alexander Graham Bell's wife was deaf. In seeking to ease her disability, he tried to invent a hearing aid. He didn't develop a practical device, but he did invent "the talking wire" that became the telephone. Previously a proprietor of a rather mundane school for the deaf, he found his true self—by telephone.

Subsidiary activities may teach you more about yourself than your main pursuit. Clarence B. Randall was an excellent executive at Inland Steel Company for many years. As a sideline, he began writing and exclaimed,

"Creating a book is like an adventure into the unknown!" In *A Creed for Free Enterprise,* he revealed a hitherto unsuspected visionary side in such passages as: "This is a magnificent time in which to live.... Vast ideas are on the march.... We must hold aloft the symbol of our faith that the driving power and infinite ingenuity of private initiative makes people more happy than planning by the cloistered few."

A chance insight by another may teach you much about yourself. John Morgan came upon this statement by Dorothea Brande in *Becoming a Writer:* "The average student or amateur writer ... only vaguely knows that successful writers have overcome the difficulties which seem almost insuperable to him; he believes that accepted authors have some magic, or at the very lowest, some trade secret, which if he is alert and attentive, he may surprise." Those difficulties thwart nearly everyone, Morgan learned—personal feelings of insecurity, inhibitions in using the subconscious and conscious minds effectively, work-oriented barriers such as fear of failure, and environmental barriers such as frequent interruptions.

A major event in your life may also be a learning experience. World War II gave Winston Churchill new insights into himself, as he admitted in historical writings that won him a Nobel Prize.

We learn from our dreams, especially from repeated dreams. F. A. von Kekule, who predicted the molecular structure of organic compounds as the result of repeated "visions," advises, "Let us learn to dream, gentlemen."

POWER

Lord, let power neither dement nor corrupt me.

Few subjects perplex and plague man as much as power. Most of those who write negative aphorisms about it have never had it. Will and Ariel Durant wrote as historians: "Power dements even more than it corrupts, lowering the guard or foresight and raising the haste of action."

Yet power need not dement nor corrupt. As Robert Frost commented, "George Washington was one of the few . . . who was not carried away by power." But power is necessary, even if dangerous. Theodore Roosevelt said, "Power undirected by high purpose spells calamity; and high purpose by itself is utterly useless if the power to put it into effect is lacking."

As a manager, you possess power—power inherent in your position and, much more important, power you acquire by your competence, forcefulness, and righteousness.

> Kings detest wrongdoing, for a throne is established through righteousness.
> Proverbs 16:12

> Where love rules, there is no will to power; and where power predominates, there love is lacking. The one is the shadow of the other.
> — Carl Gustav Jung,
> *The Psychology of the Unconscious*

PRAISE

Lord, let me accept praise with grace, reject flattery

with tact, and learn to detect the difference. Help me to praise employees who deserve it, but never to flatter them.

> Said sly Fox to Crow with the cheese,
>   "Sing a sweet song for me, now, please."
> So this Crow, being vain,
>   Cawed a short, hoarse refrain—
> And dropped the cheese for Fox to seize.

"Flattery will get you everywhere," said Mae West in one of her famous lines—a wry twist to the older phrase, "Flattery will get you nowhere." Unfortunately, Mae West may have come closer to the truth than the author of the original adage.

The first challenge in offering or accepting approval is to determine whether it's sincere. If sincere, offer it enthusiastically or accept it graciously; if not, beware. Here are major signs of insincere approval:

- **Overly effusive.**

- **At least partly undeserved.**

- **Embarrassing.**

- **Puzzling.**

- **Offered too frequently.**

If the praise you most commonly offer your employees has any of the above characteristics, stop and re-evaluate. If the praise you receive from others is spiced with the above, take it with a grain of salt.

Beware also of approval that is little more than a social lubricant. When you or someone else says, "nice job," or something similar, they usually mean, "I'm glad you got that done on time," or "I don't have to worry about this anymore," or merely, "Thanks." To take this as anything but a lubricant may mean the recipient hungers too much for praise or status.

Flattery can victimize those who don't see the true motives behind expressions of approval. Although the underlying motive of praise may be sincere, some motives are less pleasant. Those who practice them will eventually learn that they are detrimental to the health of the company, the employee who is being flattered, and even the flatterer. Following are some unhealthy motives for praise:

- To get people to like you.

- To get people to do what you want them to do, even though it may not be in their best interest.

- To get people sidelined or make them complacent during a competitive job situation.

- To get their job.

Once you recognize flattery in yourself or in others, you have already applied some of the medicine needed to deal with it. A healthy dose of honesty is the best cure for those afflicted by a flattering tongue, and benign neglect is the best vaccine to ward off the effects of those who have it.

> A lying tongue hates those it hurts, and a flattering mouth works ruin.
> — Proverbs 26:28

PRIVACY

> Lord, help me be as discreet with the knowledge I have about my employees as you are with the knowledge you have about me.

Today, more is involved in the privacy issue than simple questions about what information should be included in employee records. Most major organizations follow the "Fair Information Practice Principles" established by the U. S. Department of Health, Education, and Welfare in 1973. Essentially, these principals state that (1) employers should keep no secret personnel data system; (2) employees must be able to correct errors; and (3) employers using identifiable personal data must ensure its reliability and prevent its misuse. Any data that is stored by name, Social Security number, or other element that identifies it with one employee is subject to privacy considerations and should be governed by the policy.

Procedures that limit access to the database are an important means of implementing privacy policy. In a properly designed personnel system, for example, salary information and codes used for performance evaluation will be available only to certain users. In general, users will be limited to those who need the information to perform their functions. Sound business practice, as well as respect for employees' rights to privacy, require strict adherence to such procedures, along with techniques to ensure database accuracy.

In the past, a major area of abuse of record-keeping systems has involved disclosure of information to outside agencies. Law enforcement officials, unions, insurance companies, credit bureaus, government agencies, and others who do not have the employee's permission or valid legal authority have at times been able to obtain information from employers.

Except for court orders and other requests with which employers must by law comply, employers should firmly reject requests for information about employees unless the employee consents. Employees expect that information given to employers will be treated with respect and not divulged outside the company.

> Do not betray another man's confidence, or he who hears it may shame you and you will never lose your bad reputation.
> — Proverbs 25:9–10

PROBLEM-SOLVING

Lord, teach me to solve problems.

Choosing courses of action that provide maximum benefit within acceptable limits of risk is the essence of successful problem solving.

To solve problems:

1. **Establish objectives.** "Solve the problem," is too general a goal. What is the problem? What causes it? Why and how did the problem arise? How can I solve it? Answers to those questions will enable you to set meaningful objectives.

2. **Generate the alternatives.** Don't settle for the first solution that occurs to you. You may end up using it, but

think of others before deciding. You may be able to meld the best features of two or three and find a better course of action.

3. **Examine possible adverse consequences.** Avoid creating new problems with solutions to old ones. A textile firm hired a behavioral scientist to help motivate employees to higher productivity. Lower productivity resulted because employees resented a stranger telling them how to do their work. But an ex-foreman recalled from retirement achieved what the scientist could not.

Solomon advises that patience is an important aspect of problem-solving.

> Through patience a ruler can be persuaded, and a gentle tongue can break a bone. — Proverbs 25:15

Lord, keep reminding me that working with people is not impossible, even though at times it is very difficult.

There are two ways to get others to do what you want: compulsion or persuasion. Compulsion is closely related to slavery. Persuasion is the method of free people.

To persuade requires an understanding of what motivates people—a practical knowledge of human nature. In answer to the question, What is the most essential thing for a manager to know about human nature? two-thirds of the psychologists surveyed said that an understanding of what makes people think, feel, and act as they do is uppermost.

In the MOTIVATION category we go into this more, but for practice, consider how you would cope with a common type, the know-it-all. Here are suggestions:

1. In as much detail as possible, describe in writing the behavior of this individual.

2. Write briefly why you believe the person thinks, feels, and behaves the way he or she does.

3. Objectively consider your own interactions with the person. When were the results better? Worse? Why? Write all this down in detail. When you analyze the confrontations, particularly the more successful ones, you will probably discover that the interactions were better because you had done your homework, avoided flat contradictions, and disagreed indirectly, if at all.

So you now have clues as to how to act in your next encounter:

First, prepare thoroughly before the meeting. Above all, check all your facts for accuracy. Avoid gaps in your information, if at all possible. If you can't learn the answer to something in advance, ask your manager before the meeting. If he or she has the answer, great. If not, report where you hope to find it. Not knowing something—anything—irritates a know-it-all, so disarm the person quickly.

Second, listen carefully and repeat to the know-it-all his or her main points. This will help minimize the tendency to over-explain, which know-it-alls are prone to do.

Third, don't over-explain and be a know-it-all yourself—and don't be dogmatic.

Fourth, ask questions to raise doubts if you disagree. You don't want to equivocate, but neither do you want to disagree directly.

Fifth, choose to subordinate yourself, if all else fails, to avoid an explosion and perhaps build a more equal relationship for the future.

> A man of knowledge uses words with restraint, and a man of understanding is even-tempered. — Proverbs 17:27

Lord, let me not stew over problems; let me solve them.

The human tendency to fuss and fret often leads to failure in problem-solving. Stewing contributes to a compelling interest in a limited area, coupled with a compulsion to achieve many and rapid successes within it. Too much pressure from the employer may result in such an impulse, but the usual cause lies within the individual. Excessive competitive drive and ambition also may lead to this state.

Dr. Jerome Bruner of Harvard University has described four traits that may result from over-motivation.

1. A damaging tendency to narrow the field of observation. If you are afflicted with this trait, you tend to look for and recognize only those clues that seem immediately relevant to the specific problem, passing up less obvious ideas that might lead to a more novel and creative solution.

2. A tendency to abandon trial and error. Those who fail to consider a number of possible alternatives get stuck on the first plausible one encountered.

3. A failure to be generic in observations. Good problem-solvers are able to see and list the basic attributes of the problem on which they are working.

4. A failure to see possible applications of information that aren't directly related. Good problem-solvers are able to apply to the problem information that is not directly related to it. They don't become too literal.

Above all, relax; you can't win them all. No one is expected to solve every problem. Furthermore, few people can stand the pace of unending problem-solving. Two of the most restlessly innovative men in history—Alexander the Great of Macedonia and Peter the Great of Russia—died, burned out, at ages thirty-three and forty-three, respectively.

And guard against compulsion. Excessive intensity develops gradually; its victims are often unaware of it. A normal interest in a subject grows imperceptibly into a passion. Michael Faraday, the English physicist and chemist who discovered electromagnetic induction, may have suffered from this defect. During several periods he stewed himself into insanity. He overcame the compulsion through long periods of rest and by turning to other challenges. You can take advantage of similar cures. Take comfort in the fact that compulsions rarely lead to such extremes as in Faraday's case.

Stewing also results from overlooking the "obvious." The late Professor John E. Arnold of Stanford University pointed out that when we tag familiar objects or actions as "obvious" such a label soon degenerates into "trivial," and thus we lose the ability to examine the familiar clearly.

According to Professor Arnold, stewing builds the following fuss-and-fret barriers:

- Failure to use all the senses in observing.

- Failure to distinguish between cause and effect.

- False conclusions drawn because of conceptualizations based on superficial likenesses.

- Inability to define terms.

- Failure to see the "trees for the forest."
- Failure to relate the problem to the environment.
- Difficulty in seeing remote relationships.
- Inability to see or find so-called trivial clues that solve big problems.

When you suffer from fuss-and-fret blocks, you can overcome them in ways such as these:

- Counteract the symptoms of the barrier. Be conscious of your own reactions to what seems to be a familiar problem, and be aware of the ways in which such a reaction manifests itself.
- Take your time in reaching conclusions. An individual with a fuss-and-fret block tends to short-circuit and jump to conclusions too rapidly.
- Watch out for the routine. This does not mean entirely avoiding routine solutions. Consider them, but look further. In short, be suspicious of ordinary answers.

A peaceful state of mind is a prerequisite to creative problem-solving, and an unfailing trust in God is the only way to achieve genuine peace.

> Do not fret because of evil men
>   or be envious of those who do wrong;
> for like the grass they will soon wither,
>   like green plants they will soon die away.
> Trust in the Lord and do good;
>   dwell in the land and enjoy safe pasture.
> Delight yourself in the Lord
>   and he will give you the desires of your heart.

> Commit your way to the Lord;
> > trust in him and he will do this:
> He will make your righteousness shine like the dawn,
> > the justice of your cause like the noonday sun.
> Be still before the Lord and wait patiently for him;
> > do not fret when men succeed in their ways,
> > when they carry out their wicked schemes.
> Refrain from anger and turn from wrath;
> > do not fret—it leads only to evil.
>
> — Psalm 37:1–8

Lord, give me discipline and focused awareness, the most important factors in the act of creation.

Basically, we solve problems in two ways.

One is to start with the known, existing idea, then select one of its attributes and change it to make it into something new. Suppose you make typewriters and want to get ahead of competition. You make manual units. You decide to electrify one model. When that works well, you add right-side justification. Then you marry your typewriter to a computer. Presto! You have a word processor.

The other common way to get ideas is the opposite of the first: start with the unknown and work backward. George Westinghouse wanted to do something about train wrecks. After much study, he decided the key was better brakes. But how to get them? He had read about new uses for compressed air. From his initial concern about the unknown cause of train wrecks, he developed the compressed-air brake. He defined the problem, found the basic difficulty, found another attribute—air—and applied it to brakes.

When you take either route, problem orientation is all-important. This leads us to three steps to take in following the path to new ideas.

Know what you seek. You can't get far with general objectives such as "I want to beat my competition in typewriters" or "I want to reduce train wrecks." You will make better headway if you decide, "I want to introduce an electric typewriter that will make the manual obsolete, and at a price that will compete with the manuals."

Analyze the dominant quality of your contemplated creation. For example, the dominant aspects of the electric typewriter would be its electrification and price. Start there.

Analyze the attributes of your comtemplated creation. With electrification and price the prime aspects of the typewriter, you go to attributes that lead directly from those two qualities: An inexpensive and simplified electrical system, probably purchased from an outside vendor at first; mass production to realize savings in maufacturing costs; mass distribution to keep sales expense as low as possible per unit nd to absorb the high output; and a major national advertising program to publicize the product.

A series of questions such as the following may help you get more and better ideas: Can an idea be put to another use? Can you adapt the idea? What other idea does it suggest? Does the past offer parallels? What or from whom can you copy or emulate? Can you modify the idea? Magnify it? Miniaturize it? Can you substitute one thing for another in the idea? Can you rearrange the idea? Reverse it? Combine several ideas?

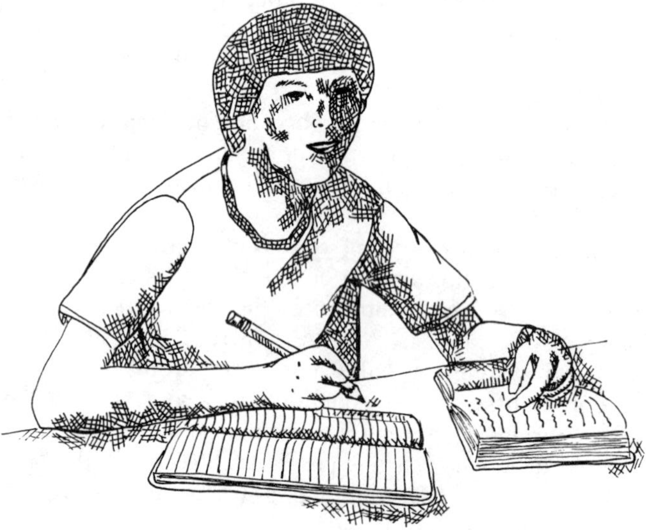

> The test of a first-rate intelligence is the ability to hold two opposed ideas in the mind at the same time, and still retain the ability to function. — F. Scott Fitzgerald, *The Crack-up*

> The dynamic principle of fantasy is play, which belongs also to the child, and as such it appears to be inconsistent with the principle of serious work. But without this playing with fantasy no creative work has ever yet come to birth. The debt we owe to the play of imagination is incalculable.
> — Carl Gustav Jung, *Psychological Types*

Lord, teach me to research—to see what everyone else has seen—but inspire me to create what no one else has seen.

People who stand still may never stub their toes, but they never will progress. "The better a man is, the more mistakes he will make, for the more new things he will try," says Peter Drucker. "I would never promote into a top-level job a man who was not making mistakes . . . otherwise, he is sure to be mediocre."

However, research can minimize mistakes. These general guidelines may help you sidestep errors:

Concentrate on what you know. Mark Twain lost much of the fortune he made as the author of *Huckleberry Finn* and other classics in financial support of unsuccessful inventions. He failed to concentrate on what he knew. A neophyte like Alexander Graham Bell came up with a rewarding creation, but Bell didn't remain a neophyte long. With the aid of research, he quickly turned himself into an expert. More than one person creative in one field has deluded himself into thinking he can be equally fertile in another; but to move successfully into a different area requires careful preparation. Alexander

Hamilton showed creativity in the fields of law, government, economics, and finance—yet he turned to new areas only after painstaking research.

Concentrate your efforts in areas where problems exist. The head of an accounting department reorganized his operation several times. He improved it somewhat; but since it never presented serious organizational problems, he largely wasted his efforts.

Concentrate on problems for which solutions promise worthwhile rewards. Example: Your operation has a limited budget with no hope of an increase, but you need money to reprint a brochure. Your creative solution is to sell some of the nonproprietary expertise of your ogranization to outsiders through an intermediary, a trade association that will charge purchasers a fee and share the proceeds with you. Yet, research reveals that your company's accounting practices will not permit the proceeds to be credited to your operation's account, but will lump them with the company's general revenues. Despite your ingenious solution, no obvious reward is visible. Forget it.

In short, **concentrate on problems whose solutions appear possible.** There is little point in your struggling to reduce the U. S. national debt. Nor is an accounting clerk spending time wisely by trying to reorganize a multibillion-dollar company, even if it needs it.

The moral: **Concentrate in areas where you have a general license to operate.** The corollary: **Take fast remedial action if you or any employee violate the guidelines.** However, do it calmly after research on why the problem developed and what corrective action should be taken. Curb any tendency to find a scapegoat. Emphasize to yourself and others that you want no one burned twice for the same mistake. And pray.

> Lord, make me able to state problems succinctly, because a problem well-stated is a problem half-solved.

This prayer is a paraphrase of comments by Charles F. Kettering, the legendary problem-solving vice president of General Motors. G. K. Chesterton adds: "It isn't that they can't see the solution. It is that they can't see the problem."

A good problem statement should include what is known, what is unknown, and what is sought.

Under what is known, consider where and when the problem is occurring, its magnitude, and why it must be solved.

Under what is unknown, list what you don't know about the problem. Ask yourself why it is occurring now and under the present conditions instead of at another time and under different conditions.

Under what is sought, go beyond "a solution." What kind of solution do you need? How can the problem be kept from recurring? Do you need an answer now, or can it wait? If so, how long? Will your solution cause other problems? If so, look further.

When we pray for a resolution to a problem and don't get it, the Lord hasn't failed us. We have failed ourselves by not defining the problem.

> Lord, sharpen my ability to evaluate uncertain, hazardous, and conflicting information.

This prayer is adapted from comments by Winston

Churchill. While we are not faced with problems of World War II's dimensions, they are still vital to our future as managers. We need the Lord's help to accomplish the following:

- Recognize the number and range of concerns to be resolved.

- Separate these concerns into manageable segments.

- Establish their priority.

- Define whether each is a problem, question, or nagging type of concern, so you can apply the appropriate analytical process. A problem is any matter involving uncertainty, hazard, or conflict. A question is a step or so below a problem. And the nagging concern may not need to be answered at once.

When we joke that we face challenges, not problems, we get to the heart of the issue of *recognition*. To treat as a problem the boss's request that we get a job done by this Friday is to overreact. Unless we cannot meet the deadline, it is not a problem; it is standard operating procedure. Even if we cannot meet the deadline, we can turn the problem into a solution if we successfully argue that we cannot meet the date unless we get another person on staff.

We need to *separate* the elements of the problem so we can get our arms around each. Otherwise, we will probably mistakenly believe that the problem exceeds our grasp.

We must set *priorities* and tackle each element one at a time for the same reason we divide the problem into component parts. In both the separation and priority issues, we must decide which we need to handle personally, which we can delegate, and what resources to allocate for each.

In *defining* the concern as a problem or something less, we apply factors such as seriousness, urgency, and growth or threat potential. This also helps us determine which require immediate action, which can be delayed for a while, and which can be tolerated.

> The blessing of the Lord brings wealth, and he adds no trouble to it.
> — Proverbs 10:22

Lord, help me find your solutions in those places where I might not think to look.

In the spring of 1879 Louis Pasteur was studying chicken cholera. He had prepared cultures of the bacillus, but his work was interrupted, and all summer long the cultures remained unattended in the laboratory. In early autumn, Pasteur resumed his experiments. He injected a number of chickens with the bacillus; unexpectedly, they became slightly ill and soon recovered. Pasteur concluded that the old cultures had spoiled, and he obtained a new culture of virulent bacilli from chickens afflicted by a current outbreak of cholera. He also bought a new batch of chickens and injected both lots with the fresh culture. All the new-bought chicks died; but the old chicks, which had already been injected once with the supposedly ineffective culture, survived. Pasteur had discovered the principal of vaccination against many diseases, heretofore confined only to smallpox.

Charles Goodyear had long sought a method to make rubber usable at all temperatures. In a seeming accident, he happened upon the vulcanizing method.

National Cash Register (NCR) researchers happened upon a microscopic encapsulating process that today has many important uses in photography, medicine, and electronics.

These solutions are what Horace Walpole, in 1754, termed "serendipity"—the faculty for making desirable discoveries when not strictly in search of them.

In all these (and many other) cases, the investigators had been hunting for years for a solution to a problem. Yes, their success resulted a little from luck, but much more from their own patience. The beneficiaries of serendipity are observant people, ever alert for creative solutions to problems.

Peter Drucker, the management philosopher and consultant, describes his analytical powers this way: "I was lucky. When God rained manna from heaven, I had a spoon."

PRODUCTIVITY

Lord, grant me the energy to work hard, the will to keep at it, and the intelligence to make it pay off.

For our predecessors, the future included the clearing and taming of the wilderness, the establishment of cities, the building of highways and railroads, the development of universities, the enthusiastic embrace of the Industrial

Age. Such goals were pursued with the confidence that they were doing right and were well fitted to succeed.

Now we are no longer so sure. Once we were the leaders of change and the hope for mankind, now we fear change. The status quo is our security blanket. When we ask, "What shall be the national priorities and how shall we allocate our natural resources?" we are asking a question we never in our history had to ask, a question we never thought we'd have to ask.

This factor—more than any deficiencies in energy, will, or intelligence—gives a tentative quality to many of our thoughts and actions today. And tentativeness never has, nor ever will, tame wildernesses, establish cities, build roads, or develop great learning centers.

How can we regain the confidence that we are on the right track? By renewing our faith in God.

> Have no fear of sudden disaster or of the ruin that overtakes the wicked, for the Lord will be your confidence and will keep your foot from being snared.
> — Proverbs 3:25–26

Lord, protect me from the negative effects of change on productivity.

In 1850, four cities in the world had a population of one million or more. In 1900 there were nineteen; in 1960, 141. The world urban population is increasing at six and one half percent yearly, which will double the census of the world's cities in eleven years.

Half the energy consumed in the past two thousand years has been used in the last one hundred. Advanced nations are doubling their gross national products about every fifteen years. Within a seventy-year lifetime, five such doublings will take place. More than half the products now on our supermarket shelves did not exist a decade ago.

The shock—or "future shock" in the language of Alvin Toffler's book of that title—comes in the scarcely noticed results of that change.

Approximately 36.6 million Americans move to new homes each year, which would be like moving the combined populations of Turkey and Lebanon in one year. In New York and seventy other major cities of the U. S. the average residence in one place is just four years.

Men and women in their early twenties can expect to change jobs six or seven times during their lifetime. Instead of thinking of a career, younger people think of serial careers. And older managers have parallel experiences. A survey by Allied Van Lines shows that seventy-six percent of the chief executive officers in Fortune 500 companies relocated four or more times in their careers.

All this transience is exciting, but also disquieting. A common psychological result is sometimes near-paralysis. A person confronted with bewildering change often retreats deep into an inner shell. This factor of galloping change, the most rampant in the United States, contributes to our anemic improvement in productivity performance, one of the weakest in the industrialized world.

How can we keep our balance against the onslaught of change? Always keep in mind these four rules, paraphrased from rules of survival for people lost in the wilderness:

1. **Stay calm.** Panic will avail you nothing. The change may benefit you.

2. **Appraise the situation.** Where do you want the change to take you?

3. **Hang on to basic principles and convictions**—honesty, compassion, etc.—no matter what else is changing, because the basics never change.

4. **Have the will to survive.** Listless resignation to change will not help you prosper with the change. Seek to control it; don't allow it to control you.

Even if apochryphal, a five-word speech by Winston Churchill is worth remembering. When a very old man, he supposedly came to the podium after a long and flowery introduction and said slowly, "Never . . . never . . . never give up." And slowly, he sat down.

PROFIT

Lord, give me a healthy understanding of the importance of profit.

Profit is: 1) Pecuniary gain resulting from the employment of capital in any transaction—*Random House Dictionary*; 2) The compensation accruing to entrepreneurs for the assumption of risk—*Webster's Seventh New Collegiate Dictionary*

> The worst crime against working people is a company which fails to operate at a profit. — Samuel Gompers

> It is a socialist idea that making profits is a vice; I consider the real vice is making losses. — Winston Churchill

In freeing peoples . . . our country's blessing will also come; for profit follows righteousness.
— Senator Albert J. Beveridge

What good will it be for a man if he gains the whole world, yet forfeits his soul? — Matthew 16:26

Lord, help me keep my enterprise profitable.

In business there is more consensus on the need for better communication than on any other factor, except on the necessity for improved profits. The parallel is no accident. Good communication and good profit usually go together.

Good communication, however, must come first. Some managers actually cut back on communication—less printed media, fewer audio-visuals, and so on—with the argument that the cuts save money and thus improve profits. The opposite is usually true. Mediocre managers go along with communication cutbacks because they don't communicate well anyhow and are relieved to give the subject even shorter shrift.

Actually, communication can be improved without spending anything but time. Closer attention to the art of talking and listening will help all managers be more effective if they accomplish most of their work through others.

Oral communication is a particularly efficient way of putting across the business facts of life to employees. Nothing is clearer in today's human resources climate than the desire of people to be told more meaningful business information about their jobs and the related challenges and opportunities in the arena where they work.

We will grow and improve the prospects for profit when we share the facts of business life.

Then we have a prayer for success.

PURPOSE

Lord, I ask not to be someone to everyone, just to the One who counts.

> O Lord, how many are my foes!
> > How many rise up against me!
> Many are saying of me,
> > "God will not deliver him."
>
> But you are a shield around me, O Lord,
> > my Glorious One, who lifts up my head.
> To the Lord I cry aloud,
> > and he answers me from his holy hill.
>
> I lie down and sleep;
> > I wake again, because the Lord sustains me.
> I will not fear the tens of thousands
> > drawn up against me on every side.
>
> Arise, O Lord!
> > Deliver me, O my God!
> For you have struck all my enemies on the jaw;
> > you have broken the teeth of the wicked.
>
> From the Lord comes deliverance.
> > May your blessing be on your people.
>
> > > — Psalm 3

Lord, teach me the difference between busyness and business, between purposeless and purposeful activity.

Jesus' parable about the sower tells how a farmer scattered some of his seed along the path where it was trampled upon or eaten by birds, some on rock where it withered for lack of moisture, some among thorns where the weeds choked it, and some on good soil where it prospered. His disciples asked him to explain further, and he replied:

> "This is the meaning of the parable: The seed is the word of God. Those along the path are the ones who hear, and then the devil comes and takes away the word from their hearts, so that they may not believe and be saved. Those on the rock are the ones who receive the word with joy when they hear it, but they have no root. They believe for a while, but in the time of testing they fall away. The seed that fell among thorns stands for those who hear, but as they go on their way they are choked by life's worries, riches, and pleasures, and they do not mature. But the seed on good soil stands for those with a noble and good heart, who hear the word, retain it, and by persevering produce a crop."
>
> — Luke 8:11–15

QUESTIONS

Lord, please judge me more by my questions than by my answers.

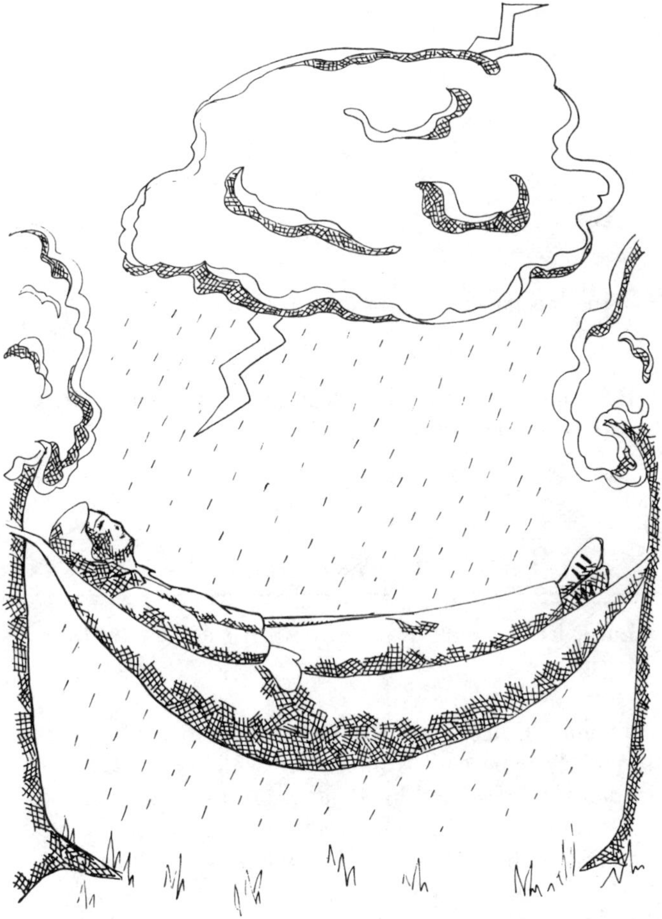

This prayer is a paraphrase of a quotation from Voltaire. Here is what some others have said about questioning:

> There are three great questions which in life we have over and over again to answer: Is it right or wrong? Is it true or false? Is it beautiful or ugly? — John Lubbock

> I keep six honest serving men / They taught me all I knew: / Their names are What and Why and When / and How and Where and Who. — Rudyard Kipling

> He's been that way for years—a born questioner but he hates answers. — Ring Lardner

> The important thing is not to stop questioning. — Albert Einstein

Remember, millions had seen apples fall, but Newton was the only one who asked why.

RELAXATION

Lord, let me relax, especially when I don't have time for it.

Thomas Edison had the habit of taking catnaps and frequently emerged from sleep with new ideas. He probably exaggerated his deafness to avoid distractions.

When living in Princeton, New Jersey, Albert Einstein regularly helped neighbors' children with their homework—in math and other subjects. He surprised his Princeton colleagues with the amount of time he spent playing the violin, an instrument he had mastered at near-professional levels.

Even during the darkest days of World War II, Winston Churchill continued to lay bricks, paint landscapes, and take afternoon naps.

Many business executives pursue other off-beat activities—magic, jazz, raising llamas, fixing power lawn mowers.

All these busy people have mastered the art of relaxation, and thus performed their major activities more effectively because they returned to them refreshed.

> If a man insisted always on being serious, and never allowed himself a bit of fun and relaxation, he would go mad or become unstable without knowing it.
> — Herodotus, *Book II, ch. 173*

> The apostles gathered around Jesus and reported to him all they had done and taught. Then, because so many people were coming and going that they did not even have a chance to eat, he said to them, "Come with me by yourselves to a quiet place and get some rest." — Mark 6:30–31

REPORT WRITING

Lord, teach me to write a report that will be read, remembered, and acted upon.

In business and industry, reports represent the culmination of many things: a problem-solving conference; a fact-finding mission; a scientific experiment; a routine progress check. Many important decisions are made on the basis of reports. Therefore, it is imperative that you write them accurately and clearly.

More than the future of an organization depends on the effectiveness of reports. *Your* future could depend on them as well. This is especially true in larger organizations where the report writer has little contact with members of upper management who have only the report by which to judge a person.

Here is a sample report of a corporation's employee communication philosophy and goals. The objectives of the corporation's employee communication are to achieve the following:

- Foster the feeling among employees that all elements of the corporation belong to the same family.

- Make employees aware that the corporation is a premier organization, with the necessity for premier work to keep it that way.

- Show management's concern for employees' welfare.

To achieve these objectives the employee communication function must:

1. Enlist the full support and cooperation of management from the top down.

2. Communicate continually and through many media.

3. Communicate in terms of what employees want to know, rather than in terms of what management wants to tell them. These wants can usually be put in the context of employee interests—job security, a sense of thrift, and interest in change.

4. Observe the following ten basics of communication:

- Use simple, clear, unambiguous language.

- Communicate regularly, not just in a crisis.

- Give reliable facts; label opinions as such.

- Recognize employee's accomplishments, contributions.

- Clarify the reasons for policies and procedures.

- Stimulate employee awareness that management is concerned about their security and well-being.

- Discuss the corporation's compensation policy frankly and often.

- Develop a sense of employee pride to be associated with a progressive corporation.

- Encourage a free flow of information up and down.

- Communicate regularly about how the corporation is doing economically; use such information to promote understanding of the business facts of life.

This document observes six basics of report writing: research, logic, simplicity, brevity, clarity, and honesty.

RESPONSIBILITY

Lord, when I give responsibility, let me be sure that it is accepted freely and that the resulting accountability is fully understood.

Responsibility and accountability are terms often confused and frequently used synonymously. Subtle differences, however, shade the meanings of the two words.

Responsibility means liable to respond, answerable. Those who impose responsibility expect accountability. However, accountability is more likely to result when responsibility is *accepted* rather than simply *imposed*. When responsibility is imposed or for some reason not accepted freely, positive results are unlikely. Accepted responsibility, on the other hand, creates more of an obligation to perform. This acceptance and sharing of responsibility is the essence of a healthy manager-subordinate relationship.

With the relationship agreed to and established, the permission to take the intended action naturally follows. This permission—involving preparation to perform and the inducement to do what has to be done—is the substance of authority derived from responsibility.

RETIREMENT

Lord, let me judge retirements, both my own and others', on the basis of personal wishes and individual value to the organization, not on the arbitrary basis of age.

What's magic about sixty-five as the so-called normal age for retirement? The answer is nothing. Nor is there magic about any arbitrary age for retirement.

Sixty-five was picked as the official age of retirement about a century ago by Prince Otto Von Bismarck, chancellor of Germany. He was establishing a social security system, the first in a major nation, to pacify those with liberal sentiments in the empire. He asked his friend, Alfred Krupp, when people in his steel plants normally had to stop working. Krupp reported that very few remained after age sixty-five, that the private plan for his employees was based on sixty-five and that it was financially supportable. That was the "scientific" way sixty-five became the "magic" age.

Retirement at sixty-five began to be introduced in the U. S. during and after World War I, largely in private plans. It became inextricably woven into our social fabric with the start of Social Security in 1935. The nation's lawmakers simply borrowed the age-sixty-five cutoff from the German system. So sixty-five acquired a kind of sanctity even though it has no demographic basis, even though longevity has increased dramatically in the past century, and even though the cutoff at sixty-five (and earlier) threatens the financial stability of Social Security and our very social fabric.

Dr. Alex Comfort is best known as the author of *The Joy of Sex*, but in his less famous book *A Good Age*, the gerontologist wrote, "What the retired need ... isn't leisure, it's occupation.... Two weeks is about the ideal length of time to retire."

Perhaps two weeks is the ideal only for Dr. Comfort and a few others, but he has a point. If you must retire, do it early and often. It's not good for your health to retire. It's not good for society because we are already experiencing labor shortages in some areas (computer and other high-technology jobs), and demographics promise they will grow progressively more widespread from 1990 on.

At sixty-five (or earlier), you don't have to stay at your same job or even at a paying job, but you should do something.

> Whatever you do, work at it with all your heart, as working for the Lord, not for men, since you know that you will receive an inheritance from the Lord as a reward. It is the Lord Christ you are serving. — Colossians 3:23-24

Lord, keep me youthful and productive even when I am past the usual age of retirement.

> Will you still need me,
> Will you still feed me,
>   When I'm sixty-four?

Those lyrics from the Beatles' 1967 song evoke the fear of aging that surfaced so strongly in that decade. The concerns expressed by songwriters Lennon and McCartney are still real.

The anxiety arises in the relationship between the aging individual and the state—which would be "you" with a capital "Y" in the song lyrics. The problem is this: Can our society afford to transfer an ever-larger share of its income to finance the health-care and income-support needs of its aged? Census Bureau projections suggest that the fraction of the population over forty-five will rise from thirty-one percent in 1984 to forty-one percent in 2009, and the fraction over fifty-four will increase from twelve to fourteen percent during the same time. After 2010, the over-sixty-five category will explode with new entrants from the postwar baby boom.

More efficient health services, more knowledge about diet, and more attention to physical fitness have contributed to higher longevity—a success in many respects, but a failure in that it strains our resources.

Unfortunately, thus far we have done little but brood over the negatives of the situation rather than take advantage of our truly dramatic improvements in health, diet, and fitness.

The answer is yes to the Beatles' question. Most of us need to work beyond age sixty-five. And we can do so with improving health. The average sixty-five-year-old today is the equivalent mentally and physically of an individual fifty-five in 1934.

On the other hand, if America can improve its productivity levels in the future, those sixty-five and over will not have to work. Most analysts foresee a productivity growth rate of one to two percent per year over the next quarter century, better than in the last ten years, but worse than the preceding twenty-five years. Productivity growth near two percent annually would lessen the generational conflict implicit in the Census Bureau's demographic projections.

> The righteous will flourish like a palm tree . . . they will flourish in the courts of our God. . . . They will still bear fruit in old age. . . . — Psalm 92:12–14

Lord, keep me from retiring on the job.

About twenty-five million people in America are officially retired. An untold additional number are unofficially retired while still on the job.

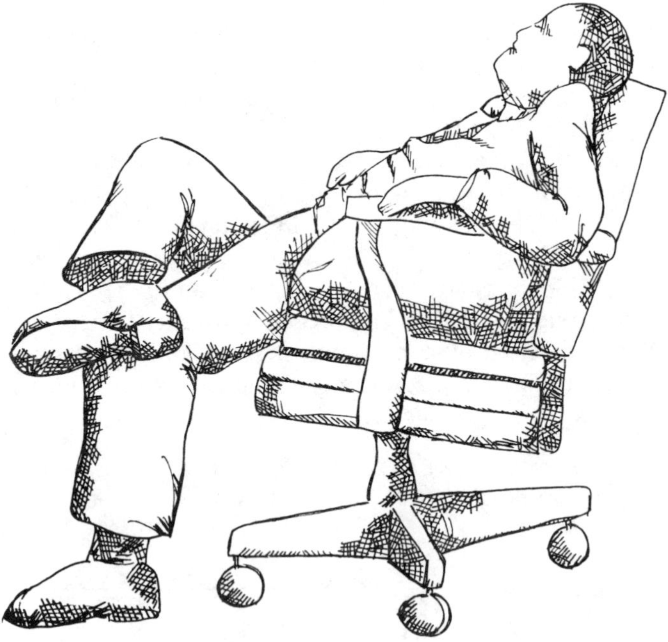

Every unofficial retiree is a tragedy, even though many would deny it. Typical undeclared retirees include:

Charley, age thirty-six, a salesman living on the customers he has developed over the last decade or so. He tells himself (and his boss) that all the golf he plays with them is necessary to maintain contacts. When one customer shifts to another supplier, he loses ten percent of his commission income but tells himself he will find a replacement at next week's golf tournament. But he doesn't. Other customers desert him. At thirty-eight he decides to switch employers, but his reputation precedes him and things get worse. Eventually, he winds up selling Hondas, with no time for golf.

Edna, age fifty-four, whose boss has just won an executive vice presidency. She gets a handsome salary increase (along with his), but, more significantly to her future, she gains access to the company's secretarial pool. Little by little, the pool people do more and more of her work. She usually asks for Agnes, a good secretary. Edna is the only one who is surprised when her boss tells her he will do his best to find her another job in the company, but that he thinks it's time for a change—to Agnes as his secretary.

Jim, age sixty-one, who's marking time until he's sixty-two. At that age he will be able to collect an early retirement pension from his employer and a Social Security stipend. His attitudes and supposed confidences to fellow employees have signaled his intentions to his boss. Consequently, he wins no interesting assignments, draws every drudge job that comes along, and is no longer even offered any committee berths. The last straw is when his boss "volunteers" him for detached service for six months with the city's United Way drive.

Alice, age seventy-one, was called "Miss Glue" at the Chamber of Commerce office, having served continuously for the fifty-three years since the Chamber was founded. She knew everyone and everything connected with the office. However, her hearing was poor, her eyesight failing, and she never could master the mysteries of the copy machine. The executive secretary regularly complained about her to the board, but they usually replied, "We couldn't get along without Alice. Besides, we have no pension plan."

You can probably name many other unofficial retirees. But please don't name yourself.

RISK

Lord, make me brave enough to face the unfamiliar and unknown.

The average individual experiences these psychological reactions to the unfamiliar and unknown:

1. **Uneasiness.** The prospect for change upsets most people until they know it doesn't threaten their status or well-being.

2. **Stimulation.** When the change is perceived as positive to their status or well-being people are stimulated by it. Lack of change, on the other hand, dulls most people.

3. **The "pied piper" effect.** People generally yearn for the changes they see benefiting others. After one successful change, most individuals are more ready to accept a second.

4. **Guarded acceptance.** If there is time to prepare for change, most people will adapt to it; they will resist, however, if no preparation time is allowed.

5. **Confidence.** Most people are confident that their energy and mental capacities are sufficient to cope with the familiar and known, but they lack confidence in their ability to deal successfully with changes to their habits and customs.

We can, however, face the unfamiliar and unknown when we:

1. Determine it doesn't threaten our status or well-being.

2. Recognize that change is stimulating.

3. Accept that habits and customs may have to be modified.

4. Negotiate, if possible, for the most advantageous circumstances in which to deal with the forthcoming change.

Yale's late William Lyon Phelps said, "The fear of life is the favorite disease of the twentieth century." Don't catch it!

Lord, let me accept the sensible risk, reject the stupid, and know the difference.

Taking risks—which means moving beyond the expectations of your peers and your boss–can prove successful if your risk-taking is securely grounded in your power and authority. But these two factors aren't the same.

Authority is the authorization you need to perform certain acts, make decisions, or commit the organization's future. You derive authority from the organization through formally delegated authority, from peers who agree on the extent of your authority, and from yourself when you assume responsibility.

The more you move from delegated authority to self-derived responsibility, the more risk you must take. When you claim no authority to perform an independent act of judgment, you disclaim personal responsibility in order to avoid risk. When you look to see what your peers are doing instead, you seek safety from their support. But when you act, even though you know "it may be my neck," you take a chance on your own authority.

Taking such a risk could be disastrous if you have no power to control the behavior of others because such power directly affects your ability to implement change or accomplish anything. Without power, any kind of authority is worthless; with power, any kind of authority has less risk attached.

The first power source is friendship. The network of social relations within the organization, both horizontally and vertically, can give you a prime source of power. Is your boss also your friend? Will your peers be sufficient friends to support you?

The second source of power lies in desirable personal traits. Self-confidence outshines all others, including the degree to which you can communicate it to others. This does not mean you must assume an aura of infallibility. Admitting your mistakes may be the best way to persuade people to trust your judgment. Other desirable traits include coolness under fire, honesty, and objectivity.

Opportunity is the third source of power. Can you get

your boss's attention quickly? Do you have easy access to your peers?

Another key power source lies in your expertise and information. How good are they? How do others regard them?

Status helps as a source for power, but not as much as in the past. The same holds true for seniority.

Finally, interpersonal skills—the ability to communicate effectively—greatly affects your power base.

> It is only by risking our persons from one hour to another that we live at all. And often enough our faith beforehand in an uncertified result is the only thing that makes the result come true. — William James, *The Will to Believe*

Lord, remind me that to get profit without risk, experience without danger, and reward without work is as impossible as to live without being born.

Managers must accept risk, danger, and effort. If we won't accept all three, we won't be good managers. Indeed, we may not remain in a managing job at all.

Many authorities attest to the importance of these factors.

Professor Silvan Tomkins of Princeton believes that "creativity without willingness to gamble is highly improbable."

Mark Twain commented: "We should be careful to get out of an experience only the wisdom that is in it—and stop there; lest we be like the cat that sits down on a hot stove-lid. She will never sit down on a hot stove-lid again—and that is well; but also she will never sit down on a cold one anymore."

Thomas Edison said genius is "one percent inspiration and ninety-nine percent perspiration."

> He who works his land will have abundant food, but he who chases fantasies lacks judgment. — Proverbs 12:11

SECURITY

Lord, grant me the only security worth having—a reserve of knowledge, experience, and ability.

Is security the first value of a job?

"No," answers the former hockey goalie, Jacques Plante. "It's the last."

For him it had to be. He explains, "How would you like a job where, if you make a mistake, a big red light goes on and 18,000 people boo?"

We may not have 18,000 people second-guessing us, but we all have at least a few. So how do we deal with critics?

By developing and honing our expertise on the job at all times.

As managers, we need to remember that our employees want a cushion against temporary unemployment and security against arbitrary discharge. When economic times are good, they also want higher pay, more interesting or pleasant work, more congenial work groups, and promotional opportunities.

Those who understand this need and do what they can to provide it for their employees will be more effective managers.

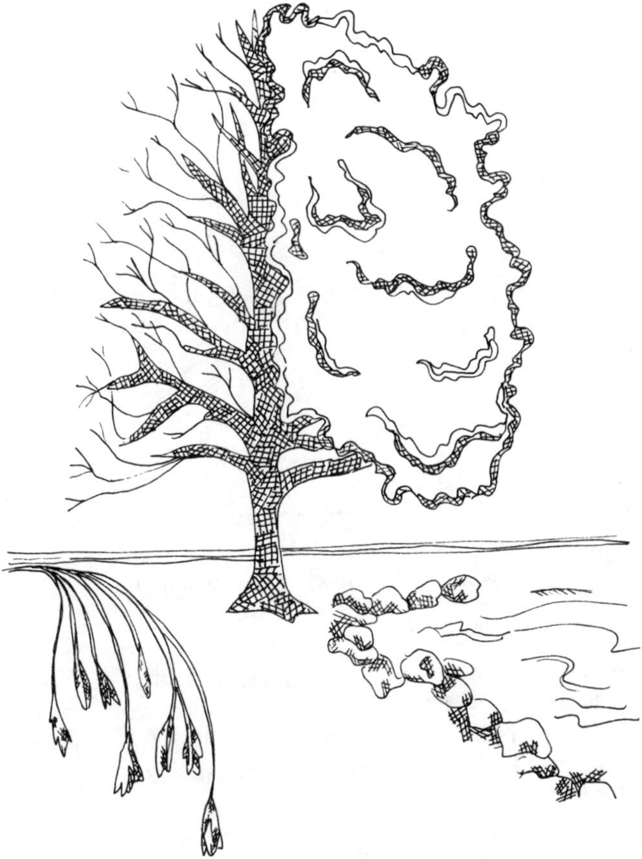

SELF-APPRAISAL

Lord, how can I tell when my work is good?

An artist won first prize for his drawing. In accepting the award, he remarked to the judge, "You know, this isn't my best work."

"Then why didn't you submit your best?" asked the judge.

"Because I haven't done it yet," replied the artist.

None of us has done our best work—yet. But hopefully in the future we will do things better as we grow and improve and change.

We can never be sure how good our work is. But we can thank God for the opportunities he gives us to try again.

SELF-AWARENESS

Lord, remind me that experience is not what happens to me; it's what I do with what happens to me.

Ian resigned on Friday. "But why are you so set on doing this?" wailed the company president. "You've been with us twenty-five years. You just got a raise. I don't understand this going into business for yourself—and into plastics. You don't know the first thing about plastics!"

"I've been studying the field." Ian launched into an explanation of his decision. He had already rehearsed it with his wife, father-in-law, and friends.

"I've always had this yen to go into business for myself. I've been able to land an exclusive license on a new process for extruding plastics. Plastics are the materials of the future. A partner is going in with me who knows the technical side. We'll both put money into the venture. I'll run the business end."

The president frowned. "And sales? You're an accountant."

He had an answer for that, too, because the objection had surfaced before. "If need be, we'll hire salesmen eventually, but for the time being my partner and I will handle that, too."

"But Ian, you've never sold a thing in your life!"

Ready for this one, too, Ian smiled. "Because I haven't sold a product in a conventional way doesn't mean I can't sell. I sell you every quarter on the best way to present the company figures. I sell all the department heads on the need to submit new reports."

Ian left the session with the president more determined than ever to prove him—and all the other doubters—wrong. He especially wanted to prove his business skills to his father-in-law. His wife's objections didn't count. Madge knew nothing about business. Naysayers spring into action every time you try anything new, Ian reasoned.

Everyone pictured good solid Ian as set for life as chief accountant for a company that had hired him out of college. He had to escape this rut. His job bored him. Inflation would soon eat the modest raise; his inflation-adjusted income from the company now was *below* his take-home pay of three years ago. And the prospect of financing college educations for his five children made him sweat. Madge's attitude toward this problem was:

SELF-AWARENESS

"Something will turn up." Something would turn up only if he made it turn up.

Ian and his partner went ahead with their plans, but in six months they had to face defeat. Their new extruding equipment didn't work out as expected. Electricity rates, a major part of their costs, rose sharply, ruining budget forecasts. Although they might have jumped those hurdles, they couldn't leap the third. As his former employer had predicted, sales proved the worst problem. Selling plastic extrusions was far different from selling accounting programs, Ian learned. The partner was too busy with production problems even to try. They hired a salesman who failed to produce, compounding their difficulties.

Why do intelligent people make errors in career planning that are obvious to almost everyone but themselves? Why do they persist, even for six months, to fail to capitalize on their strengths and experience? Many reasons account for such errors, but these four stand out:

1. **Shock and/or panic.** This precipitated Ian's move into the plastics venture. In two years he would have three children in college. The prospect so dominated his thoughts that he couldn't think straight on other matters.

2. **Outside pressures.** The challenge of education was one outside pressure, but other money matters plagued him. He and Madge lived well, because, he kept telling himself, Madge was used to an exalted standard of living before they were married and expected it to continue. He had to admit that he liked it himself. Ian and Madge moved in circles in which many of the men owned their own businesses or held high positions in well-known companies. Ian envied them. And Madge did not help his

psychological balance by making pointed comments now and then about his prosaic title: chief accountant.

3. **Inner pressure.** Ian was suffering from mid-life crisis. He dreaded doing the same old thing for eighteen more years until retirement. He saw little chance for advancement in his old company.

4. **Poor self-knowledge.** Despite his quarter century of working and his near-half century of living, Ian knew little about himself. The commentary in the next prayer suggests how he learned—and how you can, too.

Lord, teach me to know myself.

Three exercises can help you take stock and gain important knowlege about yourself.

1. Write out at least ten answers to the question, Who am I? Obviously, you might be a business or professional person. But think further. For example, I am a manager; I'm a dreamer rather than a doer. Let your thoughts wander and include both good and bad traits. Don't read meaning into the answers; just gather information.

2. List things you do well—specific tasks that have brought praise or personal satisfaction. These may be simple, even relatively unimportant, but list them if you remember them with pleasure. Then list things done unsuccessfully and/or with little or no pleasure.

3. With free choice and none of the usual limiting factors what would you most like to do? These can be of long or short duration, important or unimportant, vocational or avocational.

When you have completed the review, share it with at least one other person. Don't discuss it from the standpoint of right or wrong. Look at it descriptively.

When the new perceptions of yourself become settled and you can look at them objectively, begin to use the new insights to make decisions about your future.

Ian (introduced in the previous entry) went through the exercises, discussing his findings with his wife, partner, and father-in-law—the latter because the exercises revealed to him that he wanted to be as successful as Madge's father. He had made his fortune in a chemicals business, but, unlike Ian, his education and experience both lay in that field. None of Ian's lay in plastics.

These patterns emerged for Ian: He did need to shift focus because he had grown stale and lacklustre, but he did not need a change as drastic as he had tried. He yearned for more variety in his work and life. His worries about money, although real, were not as serious as he had imagined. His children could contribute more to their own educational expense, and Madge astonished him by saying she wanted to begin working.

The second time around, Ian gave careful thought to building a future based on his strengths and experience. He decided to start his own business as a certified public accountant. Madge took secretarial and accounting courses so she could join him as an assistant. This time, Madge's father enthusiastically supported him; he gave him business leads and even helped finance the business at the start.

The new enterprise thrived from the beginning, and Madge became a specialist in tax aspects of accounting.

Although friends and relatives can be a great asset in helping us evaluate our strengths and weaknesses, only by knowing God, who knows our "inmost being," can we ever fully know and understand ourselves.

> O Lord, you have searched me and you know me. You know when I sit and when I rise; you perceive my thoughts from afar. You discern my going out and my lying down; you are familiar with all my ways. Before a word is on my tongue you know it completely, O Lord. — Psalm 139:1–4

SELF-CONFIDENCE

Lord, let me count my chickens only after they have hatched.

Probably the most notorious example of counting chickens before they were hatched occurred in 1948 when the *Chicago Tribune* prematurely ran a headline story announcing Thomas Dewey's victory over Harry Truman for the United States presidency. Even more serious than the erroneous story was the response of the Dewey campaign staff. Thinking they would win, they let down and allowed complacency to overtake them.

Unconscious or (more rarely) conscious complacency leads to most errors in chick-counting. Chuck thought he had the job of general foreman sewed up. He considered himself the sidekick and confidante of Joe, the retiring general foreman, and he had seniority over every other foreman in the shop.

But Chuck didn't get the job. He made several errors. First, he assumed that Joe recommended him as his successor. Although Joe liked Chuck and occasionally went out with him after work, he did that now and then with all his foremen. Second, Chuck continually harped about his seniority, a principle Joe loathed because the union had plagued him with it for years. Third, Chuck assumed that Joe had the final word in picking his successor. He made recommendations, but the plant manager had the last say in selecting the general foreman. He chose Joe's second choice. (Chuck was his third.)

Although Chuck's unconscious complacency contributed to his failure to win a promotion, Bill's conscious complacency in another organization nearly did him in. Bill wanted the engineering managership but refused to ask for it. "If they don't know I'm the best person for the job without my having to tell them, I'll quit," he told his wife repeatedly. "I wouldn't work for such idiots."

"But, honey," his wife would warn, "they may not know you want the job. Can't you at least hint?"

When nothing happened for several weeks, Bill did hint and was offered the position a day later.

Some people run too hard for office. Jake didn't have a chance of becoming manufacturing manager. He made impassioned pleas for the post, to the embarrassment of all concerned except himself. He didn't seem to understand he was too inexperienced for the job. When he didn't get the position, he had to resign because in one especially emotional plea he had said he would.

Simply talking too much among peers may block a promotion, and, if you don't win the nod, it will prove embarrassing. Dr. Robert McMurry, the psychologist who heads a Chicago-based management consulting firm, advised a client: "Always give the impression of knowing what you are doing even when you're not sure." A good way to accomplish this is to make only those who need to know aware of your ambitions and ideas—no one else.

> A fool's mouth is his undoing, and his lips are a snare to his soul.
> — Proverbs 18:7

Lord, make me confident in what I believe but keep me from forming opinions that are resistant to truth and new facts.

Sigmund Freud, the founder of psychoanalysis, also bears responsibility for helping to introduce the habit-forming drug cocaine. He believed it was a cure for neurasthenia, but did not initially recognize its addictive properties and fatefully published a paper about it which he described as "a song of praise for this magical substance."

A major tire company introduced with much fanfare a new kind of tire, only to find that it fell apart if driven at high speeds.

A current theory holds that the urge to create is a matter of body chemistry. Another theory is that only people with high IQ's can be creative. Or that men are more likely to be creative than women. Or that Caucasians are more creative than blacks. Or that young people are more creative than old.

Freud, tire company managers, and proponents of the foregoing theories about creativity all held opinions found false on the basis of facts. In every instance, the fallacious opinions led to tragic results—drug addiction, fatal accidents, and pernicious prejudice.

> How much better to get wisdom than gold, to choose understanding rather than silver!
> — Proverbs 16:16

SELF-CONFIDENCE

Vanity Prestige

SELF-ESTEEM

Lord, steer me away from all vanity, especially that which flows from the prestige of my position.

> You have made my days a mere handbreadth;
>   the span of my years is as nothing before you.
> Each man's life is but a breath.
> Man is a mere phantom as he goes to and fro;
>   He bustles about, but only in vain;
>   he heaps up wealth, not knowing who will get it.
>
> — Psalm 39:5–6

> Do not boast about tomorrow,
>   for you do not know what a day may bring forth.
> Let another praise you, and not your own mouth;
>   someone else, and not your own lips.
>
> — Proverbs 27:1–2

SPAN OF CONTROL

Lord, remind me often that big doesn't necessarily mean successful.

The span of authority of any manager is measured by the number of subordinates that report directly to him or her. Most students of management believe this number should be limited in the interests of effective administration—perhaps as low as four or five and not more than eight. Unquestionably, a manager can have too many subordinates. Often this happens when superiors offer little or no resistance when the manager gradually increases staff. Eventually, someone wakes up to discover that the manager's span of control is completely out of hand.

The span of authority should be reasonably flexible, depending on circumstances such as these:

1. The manager's supervisory skill and mental acuity are probably the most important considerations. And the two usually act in tandem—high supervisory skill most frequently goes with high mental acuity. Managers with facile minds—who can concentrate, are decisive, and can shift mental gears quickly from one problem to another—may supervise more than five without strain and without impairing their decision-making abilities. Others who perhaps have equal judgment but more plodding mental habits should supervise fewer employees.

2. The general level of subordinates' intelligence is a factor. Employees who are not swift mentally require more supervision than their brighter counterparts.

3. The physical layout of the work area bears on the issue. All management responsibilities require some face-to-face encounter for good communication. If time is wasted by the layout's inconvenience, the potential performance of managers as well as those they manage will suffer.

4. Finally, the general complexity of the subject ordinarily dealt with is important. If the relative performance in the several report units is readily measurable and comparable, the effective span of authority may be increased accordingly.

And should not the manager have a say in the size of the span of control?

> Ah, but a man's reach should exceed his grasp,
> Or what's a heaven for?
> — Robert Browning, *Andrea del Sarto*

SUCCESS

Lord, let me never forget that success is a journey, not a destination.

An organization's development depends on all its employees. They are the organization.

When we feel "at home" because our working environment encourages energy, growth, satisfaction, and pleasure, we contribute to our organization's success. As managers, we have the opportunity to create this quality of working life.

Achieving it is a never-ending task. Values and attitudes of the workforce change as they keep pace with the changing attitudes in society. As managers, we must keep aware of these changes and be flexible enough to change policies to fit changing attitudes. Failure to do this will cause far-reaching consequences. Despite a few brilliant and heartening exceptions, management lagged in granting equal opportunities to employees regardless of race, etc. Consequently, the government stepped in and created the Equal Employment Opportunity Commission and other bureaucracies to force organizations to do what they should have been doing all along.

Managers must remain alert to employees' individual needs to maintain good morale. We won't achieve job satisfaction merely by adequate pay and reasonable benefits. Most employees want more—self-fulfillment in their work, more variety, autonomy, and a true sense of sharing in management's objectives.

Lord, enlighten me and help me create an atmosphere where employees work wholeheartedly *with* managers for mutually satisfying goals.

TEACHING

Lord, teach me to teach.

On-the-job instruction, which comprises the bulk of most supervisors' teaching duties, is primarily a talk-and-show proposition. Oral and on-the-spot visual communications are the most practical means of educating employees. Basically, the procedure is to explain the job, to show how it's done, and then to let the employee do it alone.

Here are a few suggestions on teaching technique:

1. **Start with what the learner already knows.** This gives confidence and reduces the possibility of nervous mistakes. Make references to and draw parallels with what your learner already understands. You must thoroughly comprehend what you teach and be able to put it in contexts meaningful for the learner.

2. **Proceed bit by bit.** Break the instruction into logical parts and teach easier portions first.

3. **Repeat—again and again.** But do it in varying ways—by demonstration, by telling, by movies or pictures if available, etc.

4. **Insist on practice.** If you teach more than one person at a time, have them practice together to help relieve tedium.

5. **Ask questions or encourage them from the students.** Their answers will tell you if you are getting across, as will their questions. If no questions arise spontaneously, ask a few yourself to prime the pump—such as, why do you think we do it this way? Can you think of other ways to do it? etc.

6. **Give encouragement.** If your learners pick up the instructions fast, be generous in your praise. If they are slack, ask yourself if you are to blame. If you sincerely believe you are not, censure those who are—but in private.

7. **Use visual aids**—examples of previous similar jobs, pictures, movies, drawings, anything else that is available.

8. **Show how the learner fits into the picture.** Indicate the relationship with others. Emphasize the role's importance.

9. **Show how the work to be done fits into the total picture.** Give the job's history. Show the use to which the work will be put.

10. **Put the students on their own, but at the right time.** Don't put this off too long, a common problem. A good way to know if the time is right is to ask. If they seem confident, go ahead. If not, try more practice. One manager says, "When they anticipate my points on the umpty-umpth time around and get impatient, that's when the time is ripe."

11. **Follow through.** Check their work, but as unobtrusively as possible. Make corrections patiently, quietly.

12. **Keep on the lookout for the better students.** You

never have too much talent working for you. During the instruction period, you usually deal more closely with employees than at any other time. Take advantage of the opportunity because it is when first—and often the best—impressions are formed.

> Instruct a wise man and he will be wiser still; teach a righteous man and he will add to his learning.
> — Proverbs 9:9

TEAMWORK

Lord, let me work with and through others that our results may be multiplied.

The manager is the most important link between the executive suite and the employees on the floor in resolving the real or supposed conflicts between high productivity and high morale. Poor supervision will quickly dissipate most of the benefits of a sound personnel program or management philosophy. Good management can offset many minor disadvantages in the work situation. Good supervision is an essential element in most employees' job satisfaction.

Recent studies reveal that productivity is not necessarily higher just because employees have a generally favorable attitude about the employing organization. Similarly, many morale-building practices have not automatically yielded better productivity. However, managers who are "employee-centered" get high productivity. Subordinates of such bosses take pride in their work; high achievers in these work groups are admired, not resented.

Managers can become more "employee-centered" if they:

- Show sincere interest in employees' problems.

- Develop employee job satisfaction.

- Give general, not close supervision, setting goals, but allowing discretion as to how the job gets done.

- Emphasize downward communication and team spirit.

- Develop a sense of participation and contribution.

- Listen to employees' complaints and suggestions.

- Support deserving employees to win promotions and pay increases.

- Coach employees to prepare for better jobs.

- Encourage improvements in job design and job performance.

- Foster participation in the problem solving process at appropriate levels of expertise and responsibility.

This last point has the potential to build as much team spirit as all the rest combined. Here are suggestions on how to do it:

1. Develop programs and policies that encourage employees to make creative suggestions, and that reward their contributions.

2. Develop philosophies and procedures to ensure that past practices aren't used as the only rationale for continuing such practices.

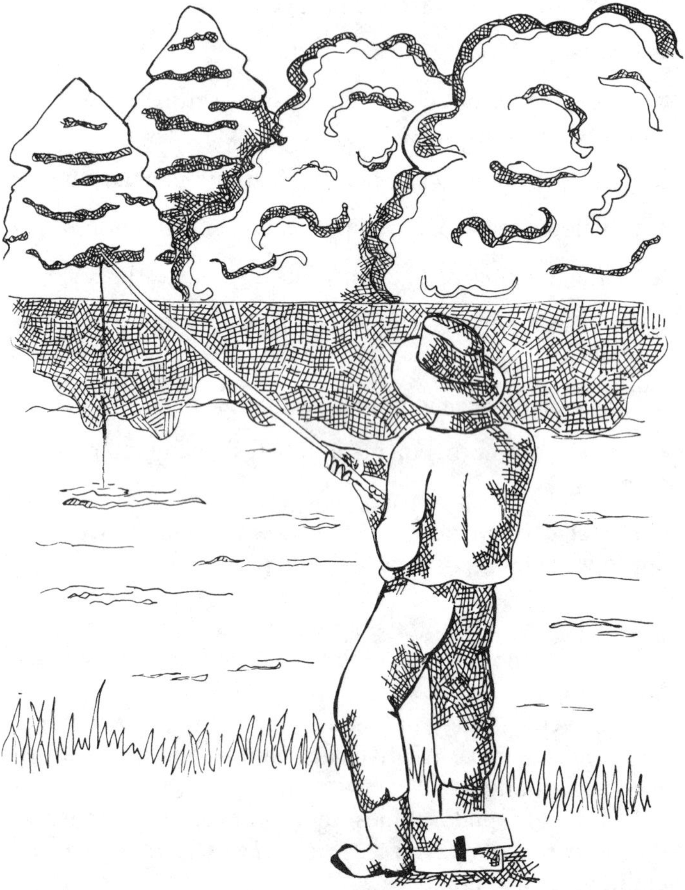

3. Adopt a nonjudgmental attitude toward new and innovative suggestions. Nothing kills creativity faster than a snap negative verdict.

When you and your team create something of quality and endurance, you will catch a hint of how God felt when he finished his act of creation as recounted in Genesis 1:25. "And God saw that it was good."

TIME

Lord, help me to use time more effectively.

"Time is but the stream I go a-fishing in," Thoreau wrote.

Time is your most precious asset. Used wisely, time works for you, getting your job done effectively. Used unwisely, time drifts away, with your work undone.

We've heard all the reasons why time drifts away: a customer who takes forever to explain his requirements; crises that take unexpected time to resolve; and interruptions—an unending phone call or the walk-in you can't get rid of. This list goes on, and you'll always have to cope with time-wasters to some extent. Yet, if you take time to save time, you can minimize even the inevitable time wasters to a surprising extent.

First, jot down what you do on your job. You may discover that you've taken on tasks that are, or should be, someone else's responsibility. You may also find that, by letting yourself get immersed in details, you're neglecting some of what should be your major activities.

Or you may even learn you're concentrating too much on only those tasks that interest you.

Once you've committed to paper the real nature of your job, you can redefine your true objectives, confine yourself to those goals alone, and decide what you can delegate. In general, you can delegate if a task is repetitive or routine, if it can be performed by a subordinate with the ability and information to handle it, or if it can be handled in only one clear-cut way that can be taught.

A timetable need not be complicated. Simply take an 8 1/2 by 11-inch sheet of paper and divide it into three columns with the following headings: To Do; Doing; Done. Use a new sheet for each week, and date it for your records. On Monday morning, list all the tasks you hope to schedule for the week. At the start, of course, all will be in the "To Do" or "Doing" columns. All the "To Do" items should bear the date when you first got the assignment or made it to yourself. All the "Doing" tasks should bear the date you started work on them.

At the start of every morning from Tuesday through Friday note any change in status and add new jobs. Note the date of the changed status. At the end of the week, file the worksheet for reference on the following Monday morning and for review in about two months' time. Then, note what's still unfinished. Resolve to give those tasks top priority. You should spend no more than two and a half hours a week with the work sheet—half an hour a day.

It will take discipline to get the sheet working satisfactorily, and you must maintain reasonable flexibility; never become a slave to it. At the start, all will not go smoothly. But within a few weeks, you should be spending less and less time with it—sometimes fifteen minutes a day or even less. Knowledge of what you're going to do and a quick reference on the status of each job will perform wonders in getting them moved off your sheet.

And the interruptions? You will find you don't talk as long on the phone if your worksheet of unfinished tasks lies before your eyes as you speak.

A slow customer? You can't solve this one every time, but knowing from your early morning review that you have seven tasks in the "Doing" column and eight in the "To Do" column will encourage you to think of ways to speed the customer.

Crises that take unexpected time? You won't have nearly as many when you schedule your work.

When you have used this system for a few months, one of three things may happen:

1. You may find you don't have enough to do each day. If so, start those long-term projects you've postponed so long.

2. You may find you are truly overloaded. Discuss with your boss ways to ease the pressure. Your worksheets will help prove your case.

3. You will delegate more than you did before you started.

Whatever the outcome, you will not be the one approached by the critic Bernard Berenson, who lamented, "I would I could stand on a busy corner, hat in hand, and beg people to throw me all their wasted hours."

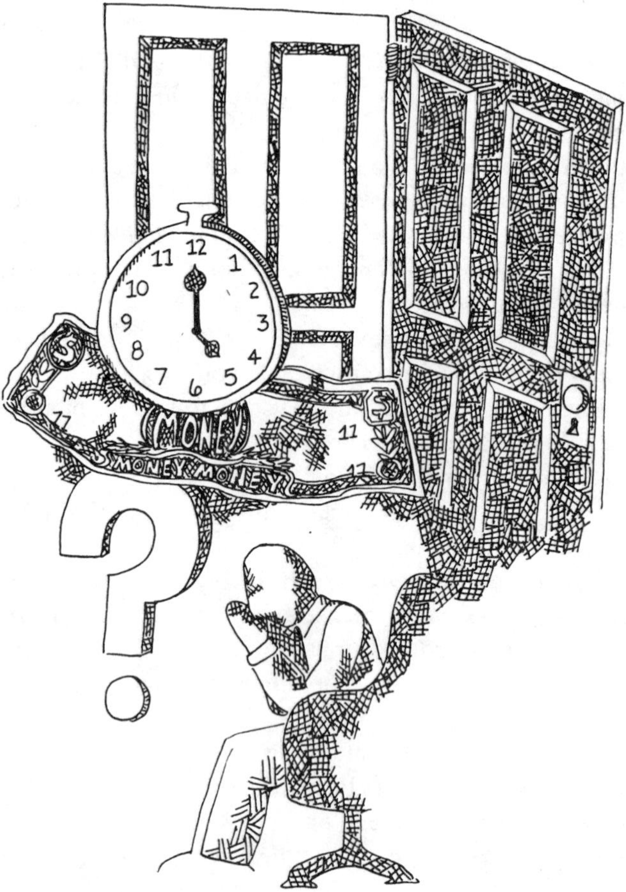
MONEY
MONEY MONEY

TRUTH/HONESTY

Lord, put ethics higher than profit in my business lexicon and fraud lower than loss.

An alumnus of a major university received this letter:

> As a result of a recent reorganization, my responsibilities are not up to the business challenge I seek.
>
> My record with a large corporation has had excellent personal growth and has been very satisfying. My proven track record shows a powerful contribution to orders, sales, and net income plus strong managerial results.
>
> The position I seek is to manage a P & L business or run a sales/marketing organization. I want something that allows me to utilize my engineering, sales, and managerial capabilities.
>
> My career has included attending nearly every major training program my employers offer, including marketing management, executive development, and international management. This broad exposure will enable me to move constructively into many different business fields. My present income exceeds $100,000 yearly.
>
> While you may have nothing available directly, any leads, advice, or suggestions would be appreciated. Soon, I'll contact you, or you may call or write me. My present employer does not know I'm looking, so it's premature to alert them.

The attached resume looked impressive. As it happened, the alumnus did have an opening that seemed a good fit with the applicant's qualifications. However, the letter and resume sounded two alarms. The first was the failure to name the present or any earlier employer, except generically. The second was the avenue through which the applicant chose to send his letters. A seasoned senior executive in his early fifties, as he claimed, does not normally go broadside via the college alumni route because he would typically use his personal network.

Nevertheless, the alumnus called the applicant who proved forceful and impressive. He readily named his current employer, a prominent organization well known for its lack of enthusiasm about job hoppers. The alumnus promised to get back to him, still troubled because the applicant volunteered names of no other employers. Furthermore, he seemed to know no one he knew in the Class of 1954 to which he claimed to belong. A check with the university revealed he had attended for one semester and had not graduated as implied.

Intrigued and suspicious now, the alumnus used his own network this time. He contacted a friend at the claimed employer and learned that the applicant had worked there, had held the job named in the resume, but had been fired for offering bribes to overseas customers.

The alumnus dropped the applicant. He didn't want dealings with someone who would bribe and give people false implications about his education and employment status.

In most books about management, ethics are confined to the preface. Here near the end, we sound an urgent warning against lying and cheating.

> A fortune made by a lying tongue is a fleeting vapor and a deadly snare. — Proverbs 21:6

Lord, let me not begrudge to others what I cannot use myself.

In every business downturn, the story is the same: many employers "discover" they can get along with fewer employees in their administrative offices even though the amount of work remains about the same.

Earl took advantage of the phenomenon. He built up a little accounting empire when times were good and "did my part" when times were tighter by letting a few people go.

"It's the only way to operate," he explained privately. "If I didn't have a few extra people on board from when business was booming, I would have to let some good people go when the next edict came along to cut back ten percent on my head count. It's common sense."

But Earl's boss didn't see it as common sense; he saw it as hoarding. After twice seeing Earl go through the cycles of expansion and contraction, he refused to okay an increase in head count during the next good phase. When he discovered Earl had found a way to get around him by jiggering the count with tricky allocations of secretarial and professional people, he warned him. Yet Earl persisted; so Earl found himself the first to go during the next cutback.

However, Earl was guilty of an even more serious brand of hoarding—suspected but not proved until after he left. Earl rarely recommended any of his people for promotion. "Needs another year or two of experience," he would say about one. "Requires close and continuous supervision," he would write about another. After Earl's departure, a re-examination of the appraisal forms revealed that the same comment sometimes appeared for several years in a row for the same person. And the employee supposedly needing "close and continous supervision" turned into a self-starter under a new boss.

In one case, an "inexperienced" person proved to be a veteran. That individual eventually won Earl's job.

> There is a way that seems right to a man but in the end it leads to death.
> — Proverbs 16:25

Lord, help me always to be honest because no one believes a liar, even when he tells the truth.

■ I have an "open door" policy but few can get in to see me because I'm so busy.

■ I am sometimes angry because that is a human condition.

■ I may exaggerate complaints, but I also exaggerate praise.

■ I avoid talking about differences between short and long-term goals because the explanation tends to confuse people.

■ I don't always reveal my motive for an action because it's usually self-interest, and that sounds bad.

■ I don't want to sound pompous by explaining where I stand on issues that affect my people and me.

■ I avoid emotions because business should not be emotional.

■ I do everything quickly, including explaining things, because time is money.

■ I do not repeat myself for that's a time-waster, too.

■ I have never told an outright lie in my life.

Why then, did my best employee just quit because he says he can't believe me?

Lord, remind me that to be persuasive I must be believable, to be believable I must be credible, to be credible I must be truthful.

Persuasion is the highest and most difficult form of communication, as was already mentioned in the section on PERSUASION. Now we can go deeper, to discuss nine basic principles of truth and honesty that underlie a sound approach to persuasion.

1. **Make sure your position is known and understood.** In addition to making it crystal clear where you stand, you also need to make known *why* you take that position. Do not let the facts alone speak for themselves. Others may not draw the same conclusions you do from the facts. Your conclusions, however, must respond to a need and be based on logic. How can your conclusions be expressed in the most palatable form? How will the conclusions look to others?

2. **Create an emotional catalyst.** Emotions persuade more effectively than facts, particularly in the short run. Of course, you must have accurate information, but you need an emotional catalyst to put them across.

3. **Take your time.** Even intelligent people have trouble with new ideas. That's why crisis communication—to head off a strike, for example—rarely succeeds. That's why continuous communication is important. Get ideas across bit by bit.

4. **Repeat and anticipate.** Repeat your message in as many ways as you can think of. In doing so, anticipate

objections that may arise and answer them before they come up.

5. **Expect resistance.** If you don't get it, beware! If people are not voicing their opposition, they may demonstrate it in more subtle and damaging ways. When you seek to persuade, you usually want to convince people to change their way of doing or thinking. Few will do so readily. Your fundamental challenge is to make them want to change.

6. **Strive for positive personal involvement.** You can most readily do this by showing people it's in their best interest to think or act in a different way.

7. **Show that the desired action or way of thinking is possible.** Role models serve well because they have already learned.

8. **State your motives frankly.** Use your own self-interest as part of your argument. Others have self-interest, too.

9. **Guard your credibility.** Here, the little things loom large—consistency, full information, the difference between short- and long-term goals. Such factors are not customarily associated with credibility, but that attribute goes far beyond just truth or falsehood. Credibility constitutes the main weapon in your arsenal of persuasion. Without it, the best persuasive techniques in the world won't persuade anyone.

> For us, with the rule of right and wrong given us by Christ, there is nothing for which we have no standard. And there is no greatness where there is not simplicity, goodness, and truth. — Leo Nikolaevich Tolstoy, *War and Peace*

WISDOM

Lord, let me use the wits you gave me, the perception you bestowed upon me, and the experience you granted me to do my job to glorify you.

Listen, my sons, to a father's instruction;
   pay attention and gain understanding.
I give you sound learning,
   so do not forsake my teaching.
When I was a boy in my father's house,
   still tender, and an only child of my mother,
he taught me and said,
   "Lay hold of my words with all your heart;
   keep my commands and you will live.
Get wisdom, get understanding;
   do not forget my words or swerve from them.
Do not forsake wisdom, and she will protect you;
   love her, and she will watch over you.
Wisdom is supreme, therefore get wisdom.
   Though it cost all you have, get understanding.
Esteem her, and she will exalt you;
   embrace her, and she will honor you.
She will set a garland of grace on your head
   and present you with a crown of splendor. . . ."
When you walk, your steps will not be hampered;
   when you run, you will not stumble. . . .
Do not set foot on the path of the wicked
   or walk in the way of evil men.
                                   — Proverbs 4:1–9, 12, 14

Lord, teach me to use the gifts I have, because I'll never be able to use those I lack.

Discipline and focused awareness have led to all the good accomplishments in this world.

Two things are essential: First is the acute awareness of problems. Second is the discipline to keep looking for an answer.

Untold thousands, perhaps millions, go through life as square pegs in round holes. Some are unaware that they are in the wrong jobs. Others lack the discipline to change even though they may be aware of the misapplication of their skills.

Lord, assist me in carrying out my own, not someone else's, functions and responsibilities. Also, aid me as a creative manager by keeping me aware of how my job might be done faster, better, and more reliably. Likewise, help me to resist efforts of others, usually with the best of intentions, to get me to stray from my true destiny. Finally, let me concentrate on the relevant and ignore the irrelevant.

WORKAHOLISM

Lord, keep me from all addictions, including work.

A workaholic as a boss can be either a delight or a disaster. Rarely is there any middle ground. Some employees find the workaholic's style invigorating; more find it a drag.

To a workaholic, everything is a number one priority. Thus he or she sacrifices reflection for action, proceeding at full speed in all directions. Seldom has the workaholic a reflective personality, although the workaholic often is quite intelligent. Frequently, the workaholic has an addictive personality, suffering from other addictions in addition to work—smoking, talking, etc.

Many workaholics excuse their problems with, "I can't help it," or even "God gave me this job to do so I have to do the best I can." Yes, we should do our best, but not to the exclusion of other responsibilities and priorities. This excuse implies that God entices us to do things that are not good for us. The Bible flatly denies this.

> When tempted, no one should say, "God is tempting me." For God cannot be tempted by evil, nor does he tempt anyone; but each one is tempted when, by his own evil desire, he is dragged away and enticed. — James 1:13–14

> No temptation has seized you except what is common to man. And God is faithful; he will not let you be tempted beyond what you can bear. But when you are tempted, he will also provide a way out so that you can stand up under it.
> — 1 Corinthians 10:12–13

WORRY

Lord, make my worries lighter.

> Therefore I tell you, do not worry about your life, what you will eat or drink; or about your body, what you will wear. Is not life more important than food, and the body more important than clothes? Look at the birds of the air; they do not sow or reap or store away in barns, and yet your heavenly Father feeds them. Are you not much more valuable than

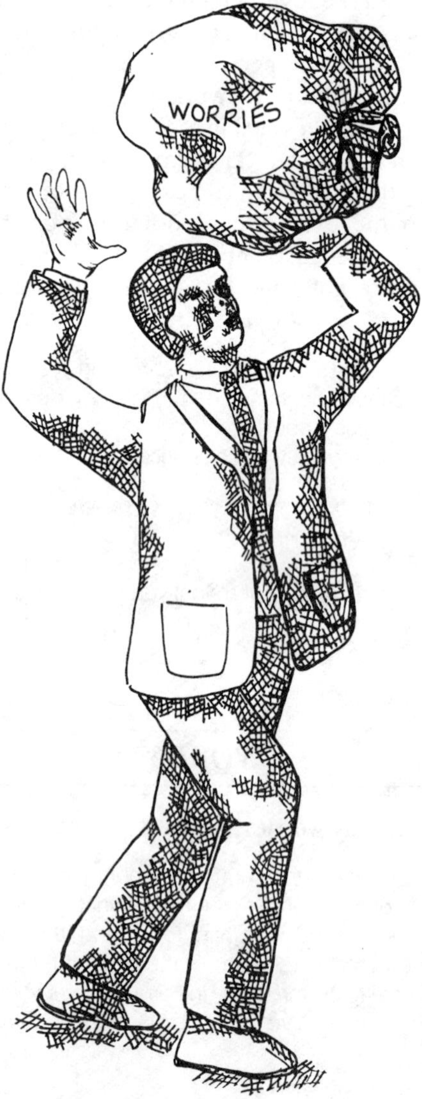
WORRIES

they? Who of you by worrying can add a single hour to his life?

And why do you worry about clothes? See how the lilies of the field grow. They do not labor or spin. Yet I tell you that not even Solomon in all his splendor was dressed like one of these. If that is how God clothes the grass of the field, which is here today and tomorrow is thrown into the fire, will he not much more clothe you, O you of little faith? So do not worry, saying "What shall we eat?" or "What shall we drink" or "What shall we wear?" For the pagans run after all these things, and your heavenly Father knows that you need them. But seek first his kingdom and his righteousness, and all these things will be given to you as well. Therefore do not worry about tomorrow, for tomorrow will worry about itself. Each day has enough trouble of its own.   — Matthew 6:25–34

INDEX

Ability, 14, 25, 66, 67, 69, 92, 105, 123, 128, 134, 164, 192, 197, 199, 221–224, 244. *See also* Competence; Creativity; Discipline; Experience; Problem

Acceptance, 42, 75, 76, 214, 221

Accountability, 90, 213, 214. *See also* Responsibility; Security; Time

Accountant, 57, 58, 82, 83, 114, 130, 227, 229, 230

Accounting, 56, 58, 63, 82, 83, 85, 112, 113, 130, 136, 173, 198, 228, 230, 249

Achievement, 64, 104. *See also* Creativity

Administration, 42, 104, 123, 124, 127, 235. *See also* Management

Adversity, 16–17. *See also* Problem

Aesop, 20, 85

Alain (Emile Chartier), 63

Alexander the Great, 192

Analysis, 25, 111, 112, 121, 128, 137, 138, 156, 157. *See also* Appraisals; Research

Appraisals, 22–26. *See also* Analysis

Arbitration, 95

Arnold, John E., 157, 192

Attention, 25, 30, 45, 51, 107, 110, 123, 129, 150, 175, 206, 217, 223, 253. *See also* Observation

Authority, 15, 37, 41, 188, 214, 221, 222, 235, 236. *See also* Influence

Awareness, 37, 131, 194, 213, 226, 254. *See also* Conscious; Perception

Beal, Orville, 40

Beecher, Henry Ward, 81

Behavior, 24, 64, 91, 93, 95, 96, 151, 190, 222. *See also* Principles

Bell, Alexander Graham, 163, 182, 197

Berenson, Bernard, 245

Beveridge, Sen. Albert J., 206

Boredom, 21, 106, 141, 176

Bosses, 32, 84, 108, 145, 156, 240. *See also* Employer; Executive; Leader; Manager

Branscomb, Lewis, 40

Browning, Robert, 237

Business, 14, 17, 18, 25, 27, 35–37, 40, 52, 62, 63, 65, 68, 70, 85, 87, 88, 93, 97, 103, 111, 112, 114, 117, 118, 121, 135, 145, 150, 152, 153, 161, 179, 187, 206–208, 211, 213, 226, 227, 229, 230, 247, 249, 250. *See also* Capital; Enterprise

Business Week, 17

Capital, 17, 18, 31, 52, 112, 135, 137, 205, 216. *See also* Business; Enterprise

Career, 29, 85, 88, 115, 145, 154, 179, 204, 228, 247

Carlyle, Thomas, 121

Cervantes, 182

Change, *See* Mutation

Chaucer, Geoffrey, 73

Chesterton, G. K., 199

Churchill, Winston, 104, 133, 134, 163, 183, 200, 205, 211

Colossians, 182, 216

Commandments, 12

Compensation, 51–53. *See also* Money; Pay

Competence, 25, 177, 184. *See also* Ability, Creativity, Discipline; Originality; Problem; Security; Time

Concentration, *See* Alteration; Memory

Concept, 26, 52, 85, 150, 166

Conduct, *See* Behavior

Conformity, 60, 170. *See also* Control; Discipline

Conscious, 67, 69, 70, 116, 132, 133, 170, 183, 193, 231, 232. *See also* Awareness; Perception

Control, 24, 27, 35, 36, 63, 64, 70, 93, 138, 150, 177, 205, 222, 235, 236. *See also* Conformity; Discipline

Controversy, 38. *See also* Crises; Doubt; Grievance; Risk

Cooper, Thomas, 81

Cowardice, 98, 102. *See also* Worry

Creativity, 64, 66–69, 71–75, 91, 135, 136, 147, 166, 198, 223, 233, 243. *See also* Ability; Achievement; Competence; Innovation; Originality

Credibility, 35, 48, 50, 75, 80, 108, 110, 150, 163, 252. *See also* Ethics; Honesty; Trust; Truth

Credit, 75–78, 179, 188

Crises, 49, 243, 245. *See also* Controversy; Doubt; Risk

Darrow, Charles B., 182

Dawson, William, 40

Decisions, 25, 85, 150, 153, 170, 175, 212, 221, 230. *See also* Problem; Solution

Discipline, 90–99. *See also* Conformity; Control

Discovery, 71, 131, 137, 166

Doubt, 75, 85. *See also* Worry; Controversy

Drucker, Peter, 11, 20, 40, 135, 172, 197, 202

Earnings, 52, 111–114, 180. *See also* Improvement; Profit

Ecclesiastes, 89, 158, 167

Edison, Thomas, 21, 69, 210, 224

Einstein, Albert, 210

Eisenhower, Dwight D., 163

Empathy, 45, 100–101. *See also* Faith; Friendship; Love; Perception; Synthesis; Teamwork

INDEX

Employee, 15, 17, 23, 25, 29–33, 43, 50, 51, 61, 62, 65, 75, 78, 79, 83, 96, 98, 106–108, 114, 126–128, 138, 146, 154, 162, 168, 175, 186–188, 198, 212, 213, 238, 240, 241, 249, 251. *See also* Subordinate; Teamwork; Turnover; Work

Employer, 20, 21, 28, 84, 103, 104, 114, 128, 144–147, 160, 161, 191, 219, 228, 247, 248. *See also* Bosses; Executive; Leader; Manager

Enemy, 78, 101

Enterprise, 183, 206, 230. *See also* Business; Capital

Entrepreneur, 160

Environment, 26, 39, 45, 78, 95, 136, 155, 156, 181, 193, 237

Error, *See* Mistake

Ethics, 56, 247, 248. *See also* Credibility; Honesty; Trust; Truth

Executive, 28, 51–53, 179, 182, 204, 219, 220, 240, 247, 248. *See also* Bosses; Leader; Manager

Experience, 16–18, 40, 45, 64, 68, 69, 79, 116, 131, 137, 141, 173, 180, 183, 223, 224, 226, 228, 230, 249, 253. *See also* Ability

Explanations, 49. *See also* Feedback

Faith, 100, 183, 203, 223, 257. *See also* Empathy

Faraday, Michael, 192

Favoritism, 42, 93

Feedback, 48, 105–110, 119. *See also* Explanations

Fielding, Henry, 16, 50, 53, 55

Fitzgerald, F. Scott, 197

Flattery, 184–186. *See also* Praise

Ford, Henry, 39, 134

Franklin, Benjamin, 73, 74

Freedom, 15, 42, 43, 45. *See also* Tyranny

Friends, 61, 88, 144, 145, 222, 226, 230

Friendship, 42, 101, 222. *See also* Empathy; Love

Frost, Robert, 67, 184

Fuller, Thomas, 16

Galileo, 166

General Electric Co., 67, 78

Genesis, 113, 243

Goals, *See* Objectives, Purpose

Gompers, Samuel, 205

Goodyear, Charles, 202

Government, 62, 65, 70, 109, 128, 129, 188, 198, 237

Gratitude, 115

Grievance, 50, 54, 95. *See also* Controversy

Guidance, 26, 119. *See also* Leadership

Habits, 46, 61, 65, 91, 92, 168, 221, 236. *See also* Workaholism

Hamilton, Alexander, 198

Health, 16, 22, 30, 32, 40, 93, 95, 104, 123, 126, 153, 165, 186, 187, 215–217. *See also* Medical Plans; Sickness

Hebrews, 105
Helper, 15, 105
Heraclitus, 39
Herodotus, 211
Hilliard, Robert, 40
Hodgson, Ralph, 81
Hoffer, Eric, 11, 41
Honesty, 54, 101, 145, 177, 186, 205, 213, 222, 251. *See also* Credibility; Ethics; Sincerity; Trust; Truth
Horace, 16, 202
Humor, 139, 141, 175–177. *See also* Profit; Earnings
Improvement, 87, 135, 168, 172, 204
Inconsistency, 133
Independence, *See* Freedom
Influence, 44, 151. *See also* Authority
Information, 34, 43–47, 96, 101–107, 123, 127–129, 138, 145, 146, 156, 169, 187, 188, 190, 191, 199, 206, 213, 223, 229, 244, 251, 252. *See also* Knowledge; Report; Research
Innovation, 72, 73, 134–137, 158, 164, 166. *See also* Creativity; Originality
Integration, 168, 169. *See also* Synthesis
Interview, 83, 84, 125, 153
Jefferson, Thomas, 21
Job, 14, 15, 20–22, 25–29, 32, 33, 39, 50, 62, 70, 71, 77, 79, 82–85, 88, 91–93, 95, 97, 98, 100, 102, 104–106, 109, 110, 115, 116, 119, 123, 128, 130, 133, 137, 143–147, 153, 154, 160–162, 166, 172–174, 176–179, 182, 185, 186, 197, 200, 212, 216, 217, 219, 223, 224, 227, 231, 232, 237–241, 243–245, 248, 250, 253–255. *See also* Operation
Job description, 143
Job security, 212
John, 99
Judgment, 35, 85, 108, 118, 146, 147, 222, 224, 236. *See also* Objectivity
Jung, Carl Gustav, 184, 197
Kettering, Charles F., 199
Kipling, Rudyard, 210
Knowledge, 13, 26, 40, 44, 47, 69, 74, 85, 102, 109, 112, 137, 139, 174, 178, 187, 189, 191, 217, 224, 229, 245. *See also* Information; Report; Research; Resources
Lardner, Ring, 210
Leader, 105, 151. *See also* Bosses; Executive; Manager
Leadership, 135, 138, 150, 151. *See also* Guidance
Leviticus, 32, 90
Liberty, *See* Freedom
Lincoln, Abraham, 102, 104, 121, 133, 134
Listening, 43–47, 101, 130, 133, 176, 206
Love, 42, 51, 80, 89, 100, 103, 115, 135, 144, 175, 176, 184, 253. *See also* Empathy; Friendship

INDEX

Lowell, James Russell, 16
Lubbock, John, 210
Luke, 115, 208
Management, 36, 37, 39, 40, 43, 61, 66, 74, 83, 87, 93, 109, 111, 112, 121, 135, 150, 155, 156, 178, 181, 202, 212, 213, 232, 235–238, 240, 247, 248. *See also* Administration
Manager, 21, 23, 26, 35, 36, 43, 47, 56, 58, 60, 63, 66, 70, 75–77, 82, 83, 85, 90–92, 94, 102, 105, 106, 110, 112, 119, 129, 130, 136, 144, 145, 147–150, 154, 158, 160, 167, 174, 176–178, 181, 184, 189, 190, 214, 229, 232, 235, 236, 239, 240, 254. *See also* Bosses; Executive; Leader
Mankind, 71, 203
Mann, Thomas, 62
Mark, 211
Maslow, Abraham, 42
Matthew, 14, 16, 24, 51, 78, 97, 121, 142, 151, 206, 257
Medical plans, 32. *See also* Health; Sickness
Mediocrity, 71. *See also* Ability
Memory, 44, 69
Methods, 16, 38, 39, 62, 107, 123, 137, 172, 174. *See also* Order; Simplification
Mistake, 14, 23, 53, 72, 73, 81, 102, 198, 224
Money, 27, 30, 74, 83, 87, 100, 105, 153, 158, 160, 161, 198, 206, 227, 228, 230, 250. *See also* Pay
Montaigne, 16
Morgan, John S., 32, 152, 183
Mutation, 166
Newton, Isaac, 210
Obedience, *See* Conformity; Discipline
Objectives, 12, 24, 27, 35, 37, 41, 64, 88, 92, 118, 119, 151, 180, 181, 188, 195, 212, 238, 244. *See also* Purpose
Objectivity, 23, 222. *See also* Judgment
Observation, 137, 138, 163, 164, 167, 170, 191. *See also* Attention
Operation, 35, 36, 63, 91, 119, 136, 148, 181, 198. *See also* Job; Organization
Oppenheimer, Robert, 41
Order, 17, 39, 47–49, 92, 113, 122, 136, 148, 168–170, 172–174, 222. *See also* Methods
Organization, 24, 25, 27, 31, 36–39, 52, 56, 108, 109, 118, 119, 127, 129, 143, 144, 150, 157, 171, 172, 175, 180, 212, 214, 221, 222, 232, 237, 240, 247, 248. *See also* Operation
Originality, 66, 67, 69, 163. *See also* Ability; Achievement; Competence; Creativity; Innovation
Pasteur, Louis, 201
Pater, Walter, 29

Pay, 51, 52, 59, 62, 69, 78, 79, 95, 97, 115, 129, 202, 224, 227, 237, 241, 253. *See also* Money

People, 12, 14, 18, 23, 27, 31, 38, 39, 41–44, 46, 48–51, 54, 59, 62–65, 67–69, 71–73, 76–78, 81, 83, 87, 90–94, 97, 98, 104, 106, 108–110, 112, 113, 118, 127, 131–133, 137–139, 141, 144–146, 148, 150–152, 161, 163–165, 172, 173, 176, 181, 183, 186, 189, 192, 197, 202, 204–207, 211, 215, 217, 219–222, 224, 228, 232, 233, 245, 248–252

Perception, 54, 166, 253. *See also* Awareness; Conscious; Empathy

Perfection, 51, 55, 128. *See also* Quality

Perfectionism, 116

Performance, 12, 23–26, 37, 52, 91, 105, 106, 115, 117, 118, 127, 157, 187, 204, 236, 241. *See also* Ability

Persuasion, 189, 251, 252

Peter, Laurence, 11, 81

Peter, the disciple, 151

Peter the Great, 192

Planning, 28, 35–37, 39, 83, 105, 119, 138, 139, 150, 178, 180, 181, 183, 228. *See also* Methods

Power, 13, 15, 71, 97, 111, 149, 166, 183, 184, 211, 221–223

Praise, 36, 184–186, 229, 233, 235, 239, 250. *See also* Flattery

Principles, 24, 36, 51, 53, 187, 205, 251. *See also* Behavior; Principles; Standards; Values

Privacy, 187

Problem, Problem-solving, 11, 17, 24, 33, 45, 46, 50, 54–55, 66–70, 95, 96, 98–100, 101, 106, 110, 122, 132, 133, 141, 163, 169, 170, 173, 174, 188, 189, 191–195, 198–200, 201, 22, 211, 216, 227, 228, 236, 239, 241. *See also* Ability; Adversity; Competence; Creativity; Decisions; Discipline; Security; Solution; Time

Prochnow, Herbert V., 81

Productivity, 16, 32, 61, 68, 161, 162, 172, 180, 181, 189, 202–204, 217, 240. *See also* Ability; Competence

Profession, *See* Bosses; Career; Management; Manager

Profit, 32, 35, 37, 49, 63, 108, 111, 112, 205–207, 223, 247. *See also* Earnings; Improvement

Promotion, 20, 25, 56–58, 60, 61, 83–85, 144, 153, 154, 232, 249

Proverbs, 13, 17, 18, 20, 22, 27, 31, 34, 38, 46, 48, 50, 56, 80, 81, 88, 94, 99, 101,

102, 107, 108, 116, 118, 119, 125, 126, 128, 129, 139, 147, 155, 161, 174, 175, 178, 180, 184, 186, 188, 189, 191, 201, 203, 224, 233, 235, 240, 248, 250, 253

Punishment, 64, 90, 95–97, 102

Purpose, 48, 67, 77, 96, 118, 143, 163, 164, 181, 184, 207. *See also* Objectives

Quality, 16, 17, 41, 70, 91, 123, 127, 136, 195, 203, 237, 243. See Perfection; Perfectionism

Randall, Clarence B., 182

Reassurance, 85

Recognition, 27, 42, 100

References, 148, 153, 238

Relaxation, 210, 211

Report, 14, 23, 33, 34, 90, 109, 131, 142, 147, 148, 190, 211–213, 235, 236. *See also* Information; Knowledge; Research

Research, 58, 118, 121, 128, 132, 137, 138, 150, 197, 198, 213. *See also* Information; Knowledge; Report; Survey

Resources, 35, 37, 43, 119, 201, 203, 206, 217. *See also* Knowledge

Responsibility, 14–16, 31, 33, 37, 52, 64, 71–80, 90, 91, 110, 138, 175, 213, 214, 222, 233, 241, 243. *See also* Accountability

Results, 25, 30, 64, 90, 91, 97, 106, 112, 118, 150, 168, 190, 192, 204, 214, 233, 240, 247. *See also* Success

Retirement, 26, 28, 29, 87, 88, 178, 182, 189, 214–216, 219, 229

Risk, 52, 77, 112, 134, 135, 168, 170, 188, 205, 220–223. *See also* Controversy; Crises

Rockefeller, David, 41

Safety, 42, 48, 102, 106, 108, 126, 147, 168, 222. *See also* Security

Scanlon, 32, 162

Security, 41, 168, 187, 203, 212, 213, 215, 219, 224. *See also* Ability; Creativity; Discipline; Problem; Safety; Time

Self-appraisal, 226. *See also* Appraisal; Analysis

Self-awareness, 226

Self-confidence, 67–69, 222, 231

Self-esteem, 11, 25, 41, 42, 235

Self-fulfillment, 42, 43, 238

Shakespeare, William, 77, 81

Sickness, 16, 126. *See also* Health; Medical Plans

Simon, Robert A., 41

Simplification, 155. *See also* Methods

Sincerity, 20, 45, 66, 67. *See also* Honesty; Trust; Truth

Skill, *See* Ability

Solomon, 22, 95, 189, 257

Solution, 17, 29, 88, 132, 188, 191, 198–200, 202. *See also* Problem

Stability, 71, 168, 181, 182, 215

Standards, 24, 35, 40. *See also* Principles; Values

Status, 42, 64, 88, 109, 186, 203, 220, 221, 223, 244, 245, 248

Subconscious, 66, 67, 69, 70, 131–133, 183

Subordinate, 23, 37, 142, 151, 190, 214, 244. *See also* Employee

Success, 15, 18, 20, 25, 27, 33, 77, 92, 106, 111, 116, 117, 134, 164, 180, 181, 202, 207, 217, 237. *See also* Results

Sullivan, J. W. N. 17

Survey, 29, 30, 145, 157, 204. *See also* Research

Synthesis, 166. *See also* Empathy; Integration; Teamwork

Talk, 33, 46, 72, 76, 82–84, 96, 97, 106, 110, 125, 139, 141, 148, 238, 245

Teaching, 238, 253

Teamwork, 37, 92, 240. *See also* Empathy; Synthesis; Understanding

Technology, 38, 39, 138, 165, 215

Thoreau, Henry David, 243

Time, 11, 12, 14, 15, 18, 20, 21, 23, 28, 30, 31, 33, 34, 40, 43, 47–49, 52, 54, 58, 60, 61, 65, 75, 76, 82, 87, 89, 92, 94, 96, 97, 106, 109, 117, 122, 127, 129, 131, 138, 140, 145, 146, 148, 149, 154–156, 164–166, 169–171, 174, 175, 178, 181, 183, 186, 193, 197–200, 206, 208, 210, 215, 216, 219, 221, 227, 230, 236, 239, 240, 243–245, 248, 250, 251. *See also* Ability; Competence; Discipline; Security

Toffler, Alvin, 41, 204

Tolstoy, Leo, 252

Tomkins, Silvan, 223

Trollope, Anthony, 73

Trust, 56, 78, 88, 105, 116, 151, 177, 193, 194, 222. *See also* Credibility; Ethics; Honesty; Sincerity; Truth

Truth, 76, 80, 81, 113, 153, 174, 185, 233, 247, 250–252. *See also* Credibility; Ethics; Honesty; Sincerity; Trust

Turnover, 15, 27, 106, 126, 153, 180

Twain, Mark, 197, 223

Tyranny, 42. *See also* Freedom

Understanding, 31, 46, 48, 56, 100, 139, 151, 155, 176, 189, 191, 205, 213, 233, 253. *See also* Empathy; Knowledge; Teamwork

Values, 27, 237. *See also* Principles; Standards

Vanity, 11, 77, 235

Voltaire, 210
Von Kekule, F. A., 130, 131, 183
Wall Street Journal, 17, 146
Washington, 165, 184
West, 185
Wisdom, 20, 22, 31, 56, 61, 79, 102, 128, 133, 139, 172, 223, 233, 253. *See also* Knowledge
Work, 11, 12, 14–16, 21–23, 25, 28, 29, 33, 35, 40, 43, 46, 47, 57, 60, 64–66, 71, 73, 77, 78, 88, 91, 92, 94–96, 106, 109, 115, 126–128, 132, 133, 136, 137, 146, 152–155, 161, 162, 168, 169, 174, 180–183, 189, 194, 197, 201, 202, 206, 207, 212, 216, 217, 219, 223, 224, 226, 228, 230–232, 236, 238–241, 243–245, 249, 254, 255. *See also* Employee
Workaholism, 254. *See also* Habits
World War II, 70, 183, 200, 211
Worry, 140, 156, 177, 186, 255, 257. *See also* Cowardice
Xerox, 39